The Everlasting Cat

The Everlasting Cat

MILDRED KIRK

THE OVERLOOK PRESS

WOODSTOCK, NEW YORK

First paperback edition published in 1985 by

The Overlook Press
Lewis Hollow Road
Woodstock, New York 12498

Library of Congress Cataloging in Publication Data

Kirk, Mildred.
    The everlasting cat.

    Originally published: 1977
    Includes bibliographical references and index.
    1. Cats—Folklore. 2. Cats—Mythology. 3. Cats—
Religious aspects. 4. Cats in art. I. Title.
GR725.K57 1985   398.2'452974428   85-13605
ISBN 0-87951-231-8

For
ANN AND PIP
and
THE WHITE TIB-CAT

Contents

The Everlasting Cat

Acknowledgements

I wish to thank the following authors and publishers for permission to quote from their works:

Mrs. George Bambridge and The Macmillan Co. London and Basingstoke for extracts from 'The Cat that Walked by Himself' from the *Just So Stories*; M. B. Yeats, Miss Anne Yeats and The Macmillan Co. for 'The Cat and the Moon' from *The Variorum Edition of the Plays of W. B. Yeats*; The Trustees of the Hardy Estate and Macmillan Co. London and Basingstoke for the fourth verse of 'Last Words to a Dumb Friend' from *The Collected Poems of Thomas Hardy*; Macmillan Co. for 'Dark Song' from Edith Sitwell's *Collected Poems*; Routledge and Kegan Paul for extracts from 'A Liturgy of Funeral Offerings' in *The Book of the Dead* translated by E. A. Wallis Budge, for a quotation from *Cambridgeshire Custom and Folklore* by Enid Porter, and for quotations from *The Fairies in Tradition and Literature* by Katherine M. Briggs; Associated Book Publishers Ltd. for extracts from *The Gods of the Egyptians* by E. A. Wallis Budge; The Loeb Classical Library (Harvard University: William Heinemann) for an extract from *Diodorus Siculus I* Books 1-11, 34 translated by C. H. Oldfather, and for an extract from Ovid's *Metamorphoses* translated by F. J. Miller; A. S. Barnes and Co. Inc. for quotations occurring in *The Natural History of Cats* by Claire Necker; The Harvard University Press for quotations from *Proverbs in the Earlier English Drama* by Bartlett Jere Whiting; The Gordon Fraser Gallery Ltd. for a quotation from *Demaundes Joyous: The First English Riddle Book* edited by John Wardroper; Edith and Maurice Curtis of The Christian Gospel Trust for an extract from *The Gospel of the Holy Twelve*; The University of Chicago Press for an extract from 'The Book of Baruch' in *The Apocrypha* translated by Edgar J. Goodspeed, for Washington Irvine's tale in *Folklore and Folklife: An Introduction* by Richard M. Dorson; and for quotations from *Folk Tales of England* by Kathleen M. Briggs and Ruth L. Tongue; George Weidenfeld and Nicolson Ltd. for an extract from *The World of the Witches* by Julio Caro Baruja, translated by Nigel Glendinning; Robert Graves for an extract from *The White Goddess*, and for 'Alice' from *Collected Poems* 1975; Cassell and Co. Ltd. for poems from *Les Fleurs du Mal* by Charles Baudelaire, translated by Alan Condor; Random House Inc. for material from *Irish Fairy and Folk Tales* edited by W. B. Yeats; Chatto and Windus Ltd. for an extract from *The Cat's Cradle Book* by Sylvia Townsend Warner; Pelham Books Ltd. for extracts from *Mostly About Cats* by May Eustace; Granada Publishing Ltd. for extracts from *Jubilate Agno* by Christopher Smart, edited by W. H. Bond; Frederick Warne and Co. Ltd. for two extracts from *Edward Lear's Nonsense Omnibus*; Angus and Robertson Publishers for the poem 'Frog Chorus' from Douglas Stewart's *Collected Poems*; Editions Robert Laffont for 'The Strange Story of the Cat of Mr. X' by Jean Cocteau in Fernand Méry's *The Life, History and Magic of the Cat*; Faber and Faber Ltd. for 'Esther's Tomcat' in *Lupercal* by Ted Hughes; Constable and Co. Ltd. for 'Pangur Bán' from Robin Flower's *Poems and Translations*; the Executors of the Malcolm Lowry Estate and Jonathan Cape Ltd. for extracts from *Under the Volcano* and *Hear Us O Lord from Heaven Thy Dwelling Place* by Malcolm Lowry; Martin Secker and Warburg Ltd. and Harcourt Bruce Jovanovich Inc. for an extract from *Cat and Mouse* by Gunter Grass, translated by Ralph Manheim; Colin Smythe Ltd. for quotations from *Visions and Beliefs in the West of Ireland* by Lady Gregory; Mr. James Strachey for 'The Cat' by Giles Lytton Strachey (Euphrosyne, 1905); the London Atheneum Press for an extract from *A Dictionary of Cat Lovers* by Théophile Gautier, translated by Professor Sumichrast, Harvard University; Hutchinson and Co. for 'The Dean's Story' from *An Anthology of Humorous Verse* by R. Carr Bosanquet; Heinemann Educational Books Ltd. for lines from 'A Night Encounter with an Egyptian God' by Tony Ross in *Children as Poets* edited by Denys Thomson; the Executors of Mrs. O. F.

Acknowledgements

Swire's estate for an extract from *The Inner Hebrides and their Legends* by Otta F. Swire, published by Collins Publishers; D. Van Nostrand Reinhold for extracts from the *International Maritime Dictionary* compiled by René de Kerchoue; International Creative Management for 'The Malediction' from *One Arm and Other Stories* by Tennessee Williams; a folk tale from *Mountain White Folklore: Tales from the Southern Blue Ridge* by Isabel Gordon Carter is reproduced by permission of the American Folklore Society; material from *The Oxford Book of Children's Verse* edited by Iona and Peter Opie, © the Oxford University Press 1973, and from *Defending Ancient Springs* by Kathleen Raine © Oxford University Press 1967 are reproduced by permission of the Oxford University Press; excerpts from *Poems from the Sanskrit* translated by John Brough (Penguin Classics 1968) pp. 83, 218, 222 copyright © John Brough, 1968, 'Metamorphosis' from *Fables of Aesop* translated by S. A. Handford (Penguin Classics 1954) p. 100 copyright © S. A. Handford, 1954, and six lines from Geoffrey Chaucer's 'The Manciple's Tale' in *The Canterbury Tales* translated into Modern English by Neville Coghill (Penguin Classics 1960) copyright © Nevill Coghill 1951, 1958, 1960 are reprinted by permission of Penguin Books Ltd.

For permission to reproduce illustrations I am indebted to: Plate 1, The Board of Trinity College, Dublin; Plate 2, The Trustees of the British Museum; Plate 3, Constable Publishers; Plate 4, Hutchinson and Co. (*A History of Domesticated Animals* by F. E. Zeuner); Plate 5, J. C. D. Smith, Bridgewater; Plate 6, Hutchinson and Co. (original photograph by N. Teulon-Porter in *A History of Domesticated Animals* by F. E. Zeuner); Plate 7, Zodiaque, Paris; Plate 8, Zodiaque and Peter Anker, Bergen; Plate 9, The Wayland Picture Library; Plate 10, Robert Hale and Co.; Plate 11, Department of Archaeology, Indian Museum, Calcutta; Plate 12, The National Trust (from Upton House); Plate 13, the Davison Art Center, Wesleyan University, Connecticut, U.S.A.; Plate 14, Macmillan, London and Basingstoke.

1

In the beginning

Cat said 'I am not a friend, and I am not a
servant. I am the Cat who walks by himself,
and I wish to come into your Cave'.
                              (RUDYARD KIPLING)

'The Cat that walked by Himself' in the *Just So Stories* came to the
cave, made his own terms with the Woman and retained his wild
ways, unlike the dog, the horse and the cow who accepted their
new roles as friend and servants and so became domesticated. But
contrary to Rudyard Kipling's tale, the cat did not walk unbidden
into the cave. It waited in the wilds for a long time until man
began to grow cereals and then it walked unbidden into the
granary.

Voltaire in the seventeenth century asked:

How can we be interested in an animal who did not know how
to achieve a place in the night sky, where all the animals
scintillate, from the bears and the dogs to the loin, the bull, the
ram and the fish?

He could not know that for an animal to achieve a place among
the signs of the Zodiac it would have had to attract the attention
of the stone-age hunting peoples who took the first steps towards
originating a system of ritual to mark the passage of the year.
There was no reason for them to consider a small nocturnal
carnivore such as the cat. The animals which form the signs of the
Zodiac such as the ram, the bull, fish and crabs were either
hunted or collected for food, or were dangerous animals like the
lion, the bear and scorpions, or the dog which was the first
animal to be domesticated. These were the animals which
impinged upon early man's mind and over which he felt it

necessary to attempt some magical control: ritual developed around them and later their names appear among the heavenly constellations.

The grain of truth in the Kipling story is that it is likely that the cat was not tamed or domesticated in the way other animals are supposed to have been. As soon as man began to grow cereals and store the grains from one season to the next his storage bins would have attracted and provided sustenance for a greatly increased number of rats and mice. The local wild cats would have come to hunt them and so would have begun the long and curious relationship of the cat with man.

Gordon Childe suggests that man domesticated his herd animals when wild herds were forced by increasingly dry seasons to congregate at his oases so that he was able to take advantage of their proximity to his camps. Similarly, cats which had previously been inconspicuous, nocturnal and wild would at first, without any effort on the part of the farmer, become better fed and bolder, and be seen more often about the barns. Some mother cats would decide that the barn was a good safe place for kittens, and children would perhaps have been able to make pets of some of these, especially if they had found ones that were orphaned. It is quite easy to see how a 'house cat', which is a better term than 'domestic cat', would have developed out of the innate good sense of the cat, coupled with natural selection, without man having to do very much at all.

Once having attached itself to human habitations the cat's habits and nature would be observable. Poets, story-tellers and myth-makers would see that it possessed attributes such as aloofness, silence and litheness of movement, hunting ability, conspicuous sexual behaviour and mysterious changing eyes which could be used symbolically to express mythological or abstract ideas.

Of the countries in the Middle East where cereal growing was first practised, Egypt is the one where the first signs of the cat's domestication are found. It is therefore not surprising that the cat became one of the large number of animals incorporated by the Egyptians into their religion.

The earliest religions were animistic. In Egypt the gods were first envisaged as having the attributes and form of the animal so that the animal was thought of as representing the god. As religious thought evolved the deities became humanized and more amenable to human control. They were then represented with human bodies and animal heads, and priests wore the mask of the animal to perform the sacred ceremonies of their cult.

At some time during the period of the New Kingdom, between 1570 and 1075 B.C. a draughtsman named Nebra working at the Theban necropolis had a stele or commemorative stone made. On it there is a carving of his two sons and this inscription:

The beautiful cat which endures and endures.

In Egyptian religion the cat had two distinct roles. The male cat symbolized the Sun-God Ra, and the female cat first represented a mother-goddess called Mut who later became the Cat-Goddess Bast. The myth of the 'Great Cat Ra' goes back to earliest dynastic or even pre-dynastic times and is recounted in the 'Book of the Dead', a sort of guide book buried with the dead to help them on their journey to the underworld. Said to be already old at the time of the First Dynasty in 5650 B.C., the copy of it preserved in the British Museum is a papyrus from the XVIII Dynasty, about 1580 B.C. Egyptologist Sir Ernest Budge has translated the Ra myth as follows:

'I am the Cat which fought near the Persea Tree in Annu (Heliopolis) on the night when the foes of Neb-er-tcher were destroyed.
Who is this cat?
This male Cat is Ra himself, and he was called 'Mau' because of the speech of the god Sa, who said concerning him:
"He is like unto that which he hath made; therefore did the name of Ra become Mau".
Others, however, say that the male Cat is the god Shu, who made over the possessions of Keb to Osiris.'

The papyrus shows a large cat with a knife in his right forepaw cutting into a huge python whose head he holds with his other forepaw. The cat is the God Ra and the python is the symbol of Apep, the arch-enemy of Ra. In the background is shown the Persea Tree, the Egyptian tree of life and knowledge which flourished at the religious centre of Heliopolis. Legend says that the victory of the good Creator-God Ra over the forces of evil represented by the snake took place at Heliopolis where Ra, represented by a statue of a cat, was worshipped.

The Great Cat Ra is also mentioned in the 'Seventy-Five Praises of Ra' inscribed at Thebes on the walls of royal tombs of the XIX and XX Dynasties. Number 56 says:

> 'Praise be to thee, O Ra, exalted Sekhem, thou art the Great Cat, the avenger of the gods, and the judge of words, and the president of the sovereign chiefs, and the governor of the holy Circle; thou art indeed the bodies of the Great Cat.'

When an eclipse of the sun occurred the Egyptians believed that a re-enactment of the great battle between the cat Ra and the python was taking place. It was thought of as a titanic struggle between the forces of light and dark. The people, fearing for the Sun-God's survival, would watch, shaking their sistra to frighten away the snake. (A sistrum is a musical instrument, consisting of an oval rattle with four metal rods across it). That originally the cat and the snake were thought of as being opposing aspects of a primal unity is shown by the Egyptian belief that both the coiled snake and the cat curled up in a circle represent eternity.

Egyptian drawings on papyrus dating from about 1100 B.C. resembling our modern comic strips show animals, the cat among them, performing human tasks such as herding geese and defending a fort with bows and arrows against an army of mice. One shows an argument between a cat and a jackal. The cat believes that the world is controlled by the gods, but the jackal thinks 'might is right' although it obviously fears the cat's claws when it is aroused in the cause of justice. Unfortunately the papyrus is damaged so we do not know the outcome of the argument.

The female cat in Egyptian religion was first known as Mut, the Great Mother-Goddess. She was the wife of Amon-Ra, King of the Gods. Over the years Mut gradually became assimilated with the Cat-Goddess known variously as Bast, Bastet or Pasht. Like Mut, Bast represented maternity and all that is feminine but she had a sinister aspect sometimes represented by Sekhnet, the Lion-Headed Goddess of War, Death and Sickness who was also derived from Mut.

To the Egyptians Bast represented the ardour of animal passion. She was a disturbing creature, gazing strangely from slanting eyes, with supple loins, elegant posture and animal abandon—attributes obviously epitomized by the cat and which, it was said, every Egyptian woman wished to possess.

Bast loved music and dancing and is often shown holding a sistrum in one hand and a basket in the other. The meaning of the basket is doubtful but the sistrum, a rattle which we have already seen was used to scare away evil at such times as an eclipse of the sun, was a symbol of fruitfulness. Its upright oval represented the womb and the handle at the bottom was the male phallus. There was usually a decoration in the form of a cat's head on the top of it. Plutarch tells us that this was the head of a female cat and was intended as an emblem of the moon.

The centre for the worship of Bast was at Bubastis, the capital of a province of Lower Egypt. Its remains are on the eastern side of the Nile Delta three miles (five kilometres) from modern Zagerzig. When Bubastis became the capital of the whole of Egypt, about 950 B.C., Bast also increased in importance and by the fourth century B.C. had become a great national divinity so that the cat was venerated everywhere.

The Greek historian and traveller, Herodotus, writing about 450 B.C., says Bast's annual festivals at Bubastis were among the most lavish in Egypt. People came from all over the country to attend a huge fair and crowds lined the river bank to watch them arriving by barge. On the appointed day there was a splendid procession, more wine was drunk than throughout the rest of the year and it was a time of practical jokes, buffoonery and general licentiousness.

Sacred cats kept in Bast's sanctuary at Bubastis were carefully tended by priests who watched them day and night. By interpreting the least purr, stretch or whisker twitch they were able to make predictions for which there was great demand. When they died these cats were mummified and piously buried near the sanctuary, and statues of cats donated by well-to-do Egyptians were consecrated and set up in great numbers.

In 1500 B.C. a temple was dedicated to Bast at Beni-Hassan which is on the Nile about 160 miles (250 kilometres) from Cairo. Mummified cats were sent from all over Egypt to be buried in the pit behind it. When in the nineteenth century this was excavated it yielded 300,000 embalmed and mummified cats. They were piled up and shipped from Alexandria to Liverpool and Manchester to be sold as fertilizer at four pounds per ton. Fortunately a few found their way into museums.

The method of mummification was as follows: the cat's eyes were carefully closed and its whiskers smoothed back against the sides of the face. Then it was wound in a tight mummy's wrapping which might be criss-crossed to form a pattern of two colours. Other details varied according to local custom. In some places scraps of painted linen were sewn on to represent the eyes and nostrils. In other parts of Egypt two small artificial ears, made from the mid-ribs of palm leaves, were attached to give an alert appearance to the now lifeless face. Further adornment might be provided by a turquoise collar. The mummy was then embalmed and, if the owner was wealthy, enclosed in a cat-shaped casket with crystal or black obsidian eyes, or in a sarcophagus made of wood, bronze or clay. A sculptured stone mummy case is described as having its larger sides carved to show 'a little cat sitting upright, its tail drawn between its legs in the usual attitude of a seated cat'.

As societies develop, social customs and religious ideas change and gods and goddesses must either be modified to suit the new conditions or be forgotten. This happened to both Ra and Bast. Ra became Osiris and Bast evolved into Isis, his wife. Osiris was at first a Sun-God like Ra, but he was killed by his brother Set and according to tradition his dismembered body was scattered throughout the land. Henceforth he is principally known as the 'King of the Dead'. Horus, the son of Isis and Osiris, became the Sun-God. That Isis, the widowed wife of Osiris, was derived from

Bast is shown by the fact that although depicted in entirely human form, she still carried the sistrum with its decoration of a cat's head. Similarly Osiris to whom the souls of the dead were taken was no longer associated with the cat. Yet cats were popularly regarded as the soul's guide on the difficult journey to the land of the dead and a papyrus drawing shows Bast, or perhaps Isis, leading a soul to Osiris.

In the 'Book of the Dead' the deceased petition the gods of the underworld as follows:

'I am clean of mouth and clean of hands; therefore let it be said unto me, "Come in peace; come in peace; for I have heard the word which was spoken by the Ass with the Cat".'

The Ass as a hieroglyph in Egyptian writing stood for a word meaning the old Sun-God, Ra, but asses are associated also with Set, the evil brother who killed Osiris. The cat may be taken either as Ra, or Bast. So it could be argued that 'the word which was spoken by the Ass with the Cat' represents the 'oneness' or primal unity which is ultimately behind the paired opposites of Good and Evil. Like the coiled snake and the curled-up cat which represented eternity, good and evil are united in this charming piece in *Les petit chats de l'Egypte* by Armand Steens describing cats getting into heaven. Here it is Horus, the Sun-God and son of Osiris and Osiris's murderer Set, together symbolizing good and evil, who help the cats into heaven. The description seems to be derived from a papyrus illustration:

The beautiful Amenti, goddess of the West, showed them the route, and thither they marched like the Chat Botté of the legend. A god grasped the delicate paws to guide them along the wonderful Pathway of the soul, or Ka, and the offerings that had been deposited in the tombs magically attended them to sustain them on the journey. At the confines of the sky they found a ladder erected, but the gods held it firm, and they scaled it without mishap. If on the last rung, the feline pilgrims, still timid as when on earth, hesitated, the gods Horus and Set held them each by one of their paws, and hoisted them all fluttered into Paradise.

At funerals it was a common Egyptian custom to place in the coffin a small ivory wand decorated with the head of a cat. This was to protect the soul on its journey to the land of the dead. Amulets and rings carrying cat motifs were also very popular judging from the numbers which have been recovered from archaeological excavations. Groups of figures of cats with kittens made of stone, crystal, blue marble, glazed pottery and porcelain have also been found. It is hard to know whether the Egyptians regarded these as religious symbols, as lucky charms, or as purely decorative.

Different animals were sacred in different localities but the cat, the ibis and the hawk were sacred all over Egypt. Did the Egyptian people make a distinction between the sacred cats of the temples and the pets which they kept in their homes? From the care with which they guarded the lives of their pet cats and the vengeance meted out to anyone who even by accident killed one, it is evident that a good deal of the veneration for the sacred cat spilled over on to her secular sister.

If fire broke out in a house, the family cat had to be rescued first before any attempt was made to save household goods or even people. When a house cat died at home from natural causes, all the family shaved off their eyebrows as a sign of mourning and lamented loudly for hours. Should anyone be unfortunate enough to find a cat dead in the street he would leave the scene as fast as possible, wailing and protesting his innocence as he went, to avoid being accused of killing the cat and possibly being lynched by an angry mob before he could be properly tried for the crime.

Diodorus, the Roman historian who visited Egypt during the first century B.C. has described an event of this kind which developed into a diplomatic incident:

> . . . at the time when Ptolemy their king had not as yet been given by the Romans the appellation of 'friend' and the people were exercising all zeal in courting the favour of the embassy from Italy which was then visiting Egypt and, in their fear, were intent upon giving no cause for complaint or war, when one of the Romans killed a cat and the multitude rushed in a

crowd to his house, neither the officials sent by the king to beg the man off nor the fear of Rome which all the people felt were enough to save the man from punishment, even though his act had been an accident. And this incident we relate, not from hearsay, but we saw it with our own eyes on the occasion of the visit we made to Egypt.

On another occasion their determination to protect the sacredness of the cat ended most unfortunately for the Egyptians. In 500 B.C. they were being besieged by the Persians at Pelusium which was near present-day Port Said. The town was resisting successfully and all was going well for the Egyptians till the Persian General Cambyses ordered his soldiers to search the whole area and collect as many cats as possible. These were tended carefully until the Persians were ready to begin a fresh attack on the town. Then the horrified Egyptians saw hundreds of panic-stricken cats racing ahead of the attacking army and every soldier carrying a live cat in his arms. How could the Egyptians defend themselves? To let fly with their weapons would be to kill more cats than Persians. Pelusium surrendered without another blow being exchanged.

In spite of the veneration which the Egyptians had for the cat, we are told that the punishment for adultery by a woman in Egypt was to be sewn into a sack with a live cat and flung into the Nile. A fitting end perhaps for a woman who had too successfully aped the sensuous Bast but hardly the right treatment for a revered animal.

From 1500 B.C. onwards cats occur in the domestic and banqueting scenes which the Egyptians, who liked to think that life after death would continue in much the same way, painted on the inside walls of their tombs. They offer a delightful glimpse of Egyptians at home with their pets.

In one scene a harbour-master's wife has fastened her cat to a chair leg. It is trying with its paw to release itself from the lead to get to a bowl of food which is just out of reach. In another scene a Theban sculptor and his wife are shown sitting together. A cat with a ring in its ear is under her chair and a kitten on his lap plays with his sleeve. Another painting shows a cat gnawing a bone under a woman's chair as she watches her husband playing a board game. In a painting of a banquet, of which only a fragment remains, we are fortunate to have the piece which shows a cat under a chair eating a fish. Chance also has left us a 'rough sketch' of a cat done in terracotta paint on a piece of flaked limestone. This is the material which in ancient Egypt would have corresponded to the use of charcoal and paper for a preliminary drawing today. The sketch is so freely done and catches the movement of the cat so perfectly that it is hard to realize it dates from the New Kingdom or between 1570 and 1075 B.C.

Also preserved from the period of the New Kingdom is a child's chair which belonged to the daughter of Queen Tiyi. On the outer face of the back there is a carving which shows the queen seated in a canoe with her two daughters. Beneath her chair is a large and very lively-looking striped cat.

The Egyptians seem also to have trained their cats to retrieve game on hunting expeditions. One painting dating from 1400 B.C. shows a cat retrieving duck for a man hunting from a papyrus skiff. In another scene a cat crouches in the reeds with a man who is spearing fish. A man named Mutsa, described as the third priest of Amen and Superintendent of the Treasury is shown taking his family, including the cat, spear-fishing and duck hunting. The cat is up on its hind legs by his side looking eager to go after the fallen duck.

In the tomb of Queen Aah Hotep cats are shown hunting ducks in papyrus thickets beside a river in which fish swim. This painting, which is dated about 1600 B.C., must have been the inspiration for similar scenes which have been found carved on weapon handles excavated at the ancient Greek city, Mycenae. In the Palace of Knossos on Crete a panel of faience tiles shows a cat stalking a pheasant—but this leads us out of Egypt and into Greece from whence the cat gradually spread throughout Europe.

2

A harmless, necessary cat

And the briske Mouse may feast her selfe with crums
Till that the green-ey'd Kitling comes.
(ROBERT HERRICK)

The house cat found its way into Europe from Egypt via Greece. The hunting scenes on the Mycenaean dagger blades are stylistically very similar to the Egyptian paintings in which a cat is stalking or retrieving ducks. Although the Mycenaean dagger is sometimes described as showing 'hunting leopards' the relative sizes of the 'leopard' and the duck are the same on the dagger blade as the cat and the duck in the Egyptian paintings. Coupled with the great similarity in style this supports the view that the animal on the Mycenaean blade is a cat. This does not prove that either cats or leopards existed in Greece at the time the dagger blades were made, which was between 1500 and 1000 B.C. It means only that the artist had seen them or seen portrayals of them such as those in the Egyptian paintings.

It is extremely difficult to date even approximately the arrival of the cat in Greece. The Greek farmer when plagued by rats and mice at first employed small predatory animals such as weasels, stone martens and polecats to catch them. These are easy to tame and train and are small enough to follow a rat into its hole. Unfortunately they also like to eat chickens and pigeons and have to be kept caged when not in use. The great advantage of the cat is that it *works* for man by natural inclination on its own and in its own time, and since it makes itself at home in man's barns and houses it does not have to be caged.

The cats of Egypt were sacred animals and the Egyptians were not willing to sell them. Pirates are said to have raided the

Egyptian coast to steal cats, outraging the Egyptians and resulting in several diplomatic incidents. Diodorus, writing about 100 B.C., tells in his *History of the World* that there was in Numidia (roughly modern Algeria) a mountain inhabited by a 'Commonwealth' of cats so that no bird dared nest there. He supposed that hunters captured cats from this Commonwealth and took them to Greece.

More realistic is the suggestion that the Phoenicians carried cats on their ships. Although the Egyptians tried to protect their cats, even sending missions to buy them back from Mediterranean ports, it is impossible to believe that they were always successful. From the tenth century B.C. the Phoenicians were the traders of the Eastern Mediterranean. It would have been quite easy for them, either intentionally or by accident, to have taken a cat on board in an Egyptian port and left it at another harbour on the Mediterranean coast. In either way Egyptian cats could have been quite widely disseminated to countries surrounding the Mediterranean Sea.

Such matters as the relative merits of weasels and ferrets (which are domesticated polecats) or of cats as mousers on farms were hardly topics for written comment in those days. Even later when written mention is made, there is confusion because the Greeks took over the word *gallê*, which in Archaic Greek meant stone marten, polecat or weasel, and began to use it to mean cat. By the time of the Poetic and Post Classical Greek writings, which begin about 300 B.C., *gallê* was being used with the meaning of cat. By looking at the date of a particular document it is possible to tell whether the author was likely to have meant a cat, weasel or ferret, but the written evidence is useless for estimating when the cat became the principle means of vermin control. In the fifth century B.C. Herodotus was using the Egyptian word *kattos* for a cat and Aristophanes in 425 B.C. uses this word in his plays. In his *Historia Animalium* Aristotle, who lived between 384 and 322 B.C., discussed the cat, the polecat, the marten and the mongoose together, indicating that he thought of them as similar animals.

The cat had evidently not yet completely replaced the others on the farm and as there is no word in Ancient Greek for 'purr' it is unlikely that it had achieved the status of a pet. It is interesting, however, that the playwright Aristophanes knew of the superstition, now spread throughout Europe, that it is bad luck for a cat to cross one's path. But in 393 B.C. when he wrote in his play *The Acharnians* about an animal offered for sale by the Boetian it is impossible to be absolutely sure whether it was a cat or a ferret.

The most widely known Greek tales of cats are undoubtedly those in *Aesop's Fables* which some authorities think were inspired by Egyptian tales such as that of the quarrel between the cat and the jackal. Aesop, however, portrays the cat as the natural enemy of mice and chickens and as a scheming, ungrateful character.

Pictorial evidence is a little more certain, suggesting that the cat as we know it may have been present in classical Greek times. There is a fifth-century B.C. bas-relief of the Battle of Marathon which shows a cat on a lead, but the lead itself gives rise to the question of whether the cat was fully domesticated, or whether it was a wild one which, if released, would have run away like a weasel. Another relief, dated 480 B.C., on one side of a marble block found at Poulopoulos between Athens and Pyraeus, shows two men trying to make a cat and a dog fight while two other men watch keenly. This cat is also on a lead.

It is significant that although many statuettes of children playing with dogs, cocks and goats have been excavated in Greece, none show cats treated as pets. However a cat on a funeral stele from the fifth century B.C. may have been a pet but it is more likely to have had a religious meaning. A Greek coin minted in the same century shows a cat about to leap at a bird which is held out at arm's length by a seated man. There are two Greek vase paintings, one of a man holding a cat on his arm while a girl with a parasol looks on; and another of a man throwing a ball in the air with the apparent purpose of amusing a cat which is perched on the arm of a woman. These are dated at approximately 350 B.C.

The cat's gradual spread from Greece to the rest of Europe is practically impossible to trace in its early phases. Outside the ambit of Greece and Italy, Europe was a collection of dispersed, uncivilized communities who left no written or pictorial records.

Our only evidence for the cat's existence here is provided by excavation of its bones. From skeletal remains alone it is not possible to be sure whether a cat is a wild or a domestic one. The setting in which the remains are found must also be taken into consideration. Cat bones in Bronze Age deposits of the Lake Dwellers of Europe were mixed with bones of other wild animals which had been hunted and killed and even the cat remains found in Iron Age settlements, as at Glastonbury in Somerset, are now considered to be wild ones.

We know that the cat had reached Northern Italy by 500 B.C. because an Etruscan vase painting of this date shows two women playing with a cat which they seem to be teasing with a bird. By 270 B.C. it was well enough established as a pet in Sicily for Theocritus, a Greek writer who lived and worked there, to make the comment that 'All cats love a cushioned couch'.

The Romans, who adopted so much from the Greeks, were slow to appreciate the utility of cats as mousers. Early agricultural treatises by Romans do not mention them. In the first century A.D. when there was a plague of rabbits in the Balearic Islands the Romans sent ferrets to control it. Not a single cat bone has been found in the ruins of Pompeii which was inundated by lava from Vesuvius in A.D. 79. Mosaics and paintings of cats have been excavated there but they are Alexandrian in style and must be regarded as exotic decorations, as are the mosaics at Orange in the South of France which were made about twenty years later.

However by the fourth century the cat had spread throughout the Roman Empire and Roman writings on agriculture recommended that they be kept in gardens as a protection against mice and moles. Excavations of Roman homesteads in Britain show that by then house cats were widespread from Monmouthshire to Kent. The circumstances in which these were found—for example, one in the basement of a wealthy home where it died in a fire—make it very unlikely that they were wild ones. Skeletal remains of house cats have also been unearthed at trading stations outside the Roman Empire such as at Vindonissa in Switzerland, and in Schleswig.

A harmless, necessary cat

As in Ancient Greek, there is no word in Latin for 'purr', showing that the Romans were late in making pets of cats; but domestic cats had definitely reached Gaul by the fourth century because the word *catus* appears in Low Latin there. An equivalent for this word also existed in Celtic and Old English. The Latin word *felis* or *feles* was applied both to the cat and to the weasel in the same way as the Greek word *gallê* was originally used for both. They were described as those which 'fell' mice, and in Anglo-Saxon, Celtic and Danish it is interesting to note that the word *fell* meant 'eager to slay' and 'to strike down and destroy relentlessly'.

By the twelfth century we read in a 'Bestiary', a treatise on the world's known animals commonly compiled during the Middle Ages, that:

> The vulgar call her Catus the Cat because she catches things (*acaptura*) while others say that it is because she lies in wait (*captat*) i.e. because she 'watches'.

In later medieval Latin the words for a cat were *murilegus*, *muriceps* or *mucio* meaning 'mouse-catcher' or 'mouse-killer'.

From early times in Europe the cat was regarded as a symbol of liberty. In fact the Roman world regarded the cat as a symbol of liberty before they perceived its practical value as a mouser. Its first known symbolic use by them was when Tiberius Gracchus who lived from 168 to 133 B.C. built a temple to the Goddess of Liberty in which a carving shows her holding a sceptre and a cup and with a cat as an emblem of liberty under her feet. Some Roman standards bore a picture of a cat, as did those of several barbarian tribes perhaps in imitation of the Romans. Whether the relatively few coats-of-arms bearing cats were derived from these banners is uncertain. Presumably the cat symbolized liberty because it was a matter of general observation that although domesticated it retained its freedom to do as it pleased.

St. Ives, who lived between 1035 and 1115 and was known as the patron saint of lawyers, is depicted either with a cat or as one. As he staunchly defended the legal rights of the poor this characterization may also relate to the old Roman symbol of liberty as a cat. If it was widely regarded as a symbol of liberty this would explain the expression which has apparently been in existence for a long time, that 'A cat may look at a King'. In a play called *Republica* written in 1553 one of the characters called 'People' who represents the common man says:

'Thought is free
And a Catt, they saith, maie looke on a king, pardee.'

Another very old expression: 'To grin like a Cheshire Cat' is also linked with ideas of liberty. Cheshire was a Palatine County which meant that it was part of the estate of a member of the Royal Court. As it is situated on the border between Wales and England it is likely that at least some of its inhabitants were not particularly loyal to the Crown. They would have delighted in a story that Cheshire being a Palatine County was enough to make a cat laugh, perhaps the same cat that symbolized liberty. Hence 'to grin like a Cheshire Cat'. More logical is the explanation that Cheshire cheeses were once made in the shape of a grinning cat's head. Since the real cat would be employed to protect the cheese from nibbling mice what more practical plan than to scare the mice off by disguising the cheeses as cats? This reflects the same line of reasoning which was responsible for placing 'vermin scares' in the foundations and walls of buildings. When old buildings are demolished, dried remains of cats, arranged in aggressive postures, are often found. It is presumed that their purpose was to scare away rats. Some consist only of a dried cat arranged with snarling mouth and paws raised. Others were of cats with rats in their mouths or under their paws. One found beneath sixteenth-century woodwork in a house in Southwark, London, was an elaborate arrangement of a cat with a rat in its jaws which appeared to be struggling to escape, while another rat beneath the cat's forepaws writhed upwards as if trying to bite the cat. This is a complicated and dramatic pose and by no stretch of the imagination could they be the remains of a cat and rats which had accidently died at this moment of action. In the nineteenth century an inn in Highgate Road, London, had the skeleton of a cat in the window. Firmly believed by the patrons to be the remains of Dick Whittington's cat, it is more likely that it was a 'cat scare'. As recently as 1921 a dead cat, posed with head and tail raised, mouth open and claws extended, was placed beneath the doorstep of a farm-house in Värmland, Middle Sweden, with the presumed object of scaring rats and mice away.

Perhaps because in Roman times hunting was an important part of the economy of Europe and relatively small amounts of grain were grown on tracts of land that were easily cleared, the cat was valuable for its fur before it was respected as a mouser. Cat skins were already being used for clothing at the time of Periclean Greece, which was between 480 and 432 B.C.; but like sheepskin it was worn mainly by the poor. Later it became more fashionable and, with the exception of ermine and marten, otter and cat skins brought the highest prices. These could have been from both wild and domestic cats.

By the time of the Emperor Charlemagne fashionable women were spending huge sums of money on the fur of otter and cat. To curb this extravagance he decreed in the year 808 that in all seasons and in all places it was forbidden to sell the finest doublets of otter fur for more than 20 sols, or fur mantles of cat skin for more than 50 sols.

This decree apparently achieved its purpose for after the end of the ninth century there is no further mention of fur apparel till the twelfth century. Though the decree was aimed against excessive spending rather than for the protection of cats, it was perhaps the first time that the fate of a species was affected by legislation.

As the number of farms increased cats were more often valued as mousers and were correspondingly less hunted for their pelts. By the thirteenth century cat fur in England was no longer popular. A canon prohibited all nuns, including Abbesses, from wearing any fur costlier than those of lamb or cat. About 1350 a Cornish Miracle play has Noah building an ark and his sceptical neighbours saying, 'All your labour is not worth a cat'—which is to say not very much. On the other hand, in Scotland in 1398, cats were fetching two pence each. As this refers to a purchase by the State it is likely that on the open market their price was higher.

The most convincing evidence of the value of the cat to the farmer is found in the various laws and decrees which have come down to us, setting out the penalties for killing or stealing one. Henry I of Saxony decreed in the tenth century that anyone who killed an adult cat was to be fined fifty bushels of corn, thereby showing that he was fully aware of the value of the cat in terms of the amount of corn it saved from vermin.

The legal codes formulated by Hywel Dda (Howel the Good), a Welsh king who died in 948, contained several sections dealing with cats. They embody Welsh tribal laws which had been in common practice for some time before. The chief purpose of the codes as they applied to the cat was to establish its value and fix the amount of compensation to be paid if one were killed or stolen. From 'the night it is kittened until it shall open its eyes' its value was one legal penny. From then till it caught its first mouse it was worth two legal pence and after it became a mouser and for the rest of its life its worth was four legal pence.

The desirable qualities of an adult cat were 'to see, to hear, to kill mice and to have her claws entire, to rear and not devour her kittens'. Whoever sold a cat should vouch that in addition to having the qualities already listed, it would not go 'a caterwauling every moon'. Also the cat's fur should be without scorch marks, perhaps because a cat who sat too close to the fire would not be a good mouser. If it was found to be lacking in any one of these requirements its value was reduced by one-third.

The worth of a cat partly depended upon who owned it. The King's pet cat was worth a pound. The cat of a mote-man was valued at six-score pence and that of a husbandman only 'a curt penny'. Since in the remoter parts of tenth-century Wales money may not have been readily available there was a ruling that:

'there are three animals whose tails, eyes and lives are of the same worth: a calf; a filly for common work; a cat; excepting the cat that shall watch the king's barn'

—which was worth much more.

If the cat which guarded the King's barn were killed or stolen the method of compensation was to suspend the cat by its tail on a clean floor so that its head just touched the ground. Wheat was then poured over it until the pile reached high enough to cover the tip of its tail. If no grain was available the loss of the cat was to be compensated by a milch sheep with her lamb and her wool.

Another medieval Welsh law declared that:

'Three animals reach their worth at a year: a sheep, a cat, and a cur',

and goes on to say that a hamlet should consist of:

'Nine buildings, and one plough, and one kiln, and one churn, and one cath, and one cock, and one bull, and one herdman'.

The worth of a 'cath' was one whole barn of wheat, and to make sure no one should mistake what was meant by 'cath' there was a drawing of one.

The Brehon Laws of Ireland which refer back to conditions as they were prior to A.D. 700 stated that a woman who sued successfully in the law courts could be recompensed with the confiscated goods of the defendant. However these goods had to be confined to items considered to be specifically pertinent to a woman's life. These included sheep, lap-dogs and cats.

Folk-lore from all over Europe abounds in proverbs proclaiming the worth of the cat to the farmer. Here we can give only a few examples:

The Mows Lordchypych were a cat is nawt.
                    (Early English, the Harleian MS A.D. 1470)

Old cats mean young mice.
                    (Italy)

Handsome cats and fat dung heaps
are the sign of a good farmer.
                    (Franche-Compté, France)

When the cat's gone off the mice go dancing.

This last is said to be known in every country of Europe except, curiously, Greece, the country from which the cat spread into Europe. It is impossible to assess the age of these proverbs as they would have been current in the oral tradition long before they were written down. The earliest printed book of jokes, entitled *Demaundes Joyous: The First English Riddle Book* which was published in 1511 contains this riddle:

Q. What thing is it that never was nor never shall be?
A. Never mouse made her nest in a cat's ear.

Painters showed the cat hunting or associated with farming. The brothers Limbourg put a cat in *Février* of *Les Très Riches Heures*, a set of paintings showing agricultural occupations during the course of the year which was commissioned by the Duc de Berry about 1412. In 1504 Dürer made a copperplate of *Adam and Eve* which has a cat eyeing a mouse in the foreground, and the left panel of the fifteenth-century triptych called *The Garden of Delights* by Hieronymous Bosch shows a proud sleek cat carrying off a rat.

When Chaucer began *The Canterbury Tales* sometime between 1386 and 1389 enough of his readers must have possessed a pet cat for this description in 'The Manciple's Tale' to be appreciated:

> *Or take a cat, nourish it well with milk*
> *And tender meat, make it a couch of silk,*
> *But let it see a mouse along the wall*
> *And it abandons milk and meat and all*
> *And every other dainty in the house,*
> *Such is its appetite to eat a mouse.*

The English Nunns' Rule of 1205 decreed:

> Ye shall not possess any beast, my dear sisters, except only a cat.

But the hunting propensities of the cat evidently disturbed the Irish St. Molig and he is remembered as having reproved his cat for springing at a swallow which had eaten a fly. At the saint's command both the fly and the bird were restored to life. As relaxation an eighth-century student in the Monastery of Carinthia in Austria wrote the following poem to his cat, Pangur Bán, on a copy of St. Paul's Epistles:

A harmless, necessary cat

I and Pangur Bán, my cat,
'Tis a like task we are at;
Hunting mice is his delight,
Hunting words I sit all night.

Better far than praise of men
'Tis to sit with book and pen;
Pangur bears me no ill-will,
He too plies his simple skill.

'Tis a merry thing to see
At our tasks how glad are we,
When at home we sit and find
Entertainment to our mind.

Oftentimes a mouse will stray
In the hero Pangur's way;
Oftentimes my keen thought set
Takes a meaning in its net.

'Gainst the wall he sets his eye
Full and fierce and sharp and sly;
'Gainst the wall of knowledge I
All my little wisdom try.

When a mouse darts from its den,
O how glad is Pangur then!
O what gladness do I prove
When I solve the doubts I love!

So in peace our tasks we ply,
Pangur Bán, my cat, and I;
In our arts we find our bliss,
I have mine and he has his.

Practice every day has made
Pangur perfect in his trade;
I get wisdom day and night
Turning darkness into light.

Although cats rarely appear in works of art commissioned for churches and monasteries, in the Book of Kells (the magnificent Gospel Book begun at the end of the eighth century by monks on the island of Iona) the complex intertwined design of the monogram page provides a touch of humour in the form of two cats who watch as rats eat the communion bread. However, as the cat became an accepted member of the household both as a pet and a mouser, representations of it intended for the delight of ordinary people became more common. Among the beautiful carvings with which the woodwork of both small parish churches and the great medieval cathedrals are decorated there are many representations of cats. Some are simple scenes of cats with their kittens, or catching mice. In the parish church at North Cadbury in Somerset a bench-end carving has a cat playing with a mouse at the top and a medieval mousetrap beneath it.

Many carvings show what seem to be satirical scenes which are often of cats playing musical instruments. At Farthingstone Church in Northamptonshire there is a carving of a cat playing the pan-pipes to lure mice from under a stool and another carving of a jester with a cat-face. In Hereford Cathedral there is an amusing scene of a duet, the cat playing the fiddle and a goat playing the lute. Two cats are shown dancing while a pig plays the bagpipes at Gresford Church in Denbighshire.

The story of 'Tybert the Cat and Reynard the Fox' was told in a series of three carved panels at Bristol Cathedral and carvings in the parish church of Kempen on the Rhine illustrate Aesop's fable 'Belling the Cat'. In the thirteenth-century cathedral of Tarragon in Spain a pair of carvings show first, a cat being taken on a stretcher to be executed by a rat carrying an axe, and then the cat springing to life. These are said to express the unspoken wish of humble people to see their master dead. The master represented by the cat was either feigning death or allowing himself to be taken captive in order to observe the true feelings of his servants.

Many church carvings show cats in association with women. There is a carving of a cat and a dog sitting on either side of an old woman with a distaff in St. Mary's Church, Minster on Thanet, and at Saffron Walden a carved corbel table shows another old woman with a cat on her lap. On a misericord at Winchester Cathedral an old woman holding a distaff and a bobbin in her hand rides on a cat. This latter may be an allusion to witchcraft and the emblems of spinning may be guild signs, since much of the wealth which made the elaborate decoration of medieval churches possible came from the cloth-weaving industry.

Cats were also popular as inn signs. 'The Cat and the Wheel' is thought to be a corruption of 'The Catherine Wheel'. This was the badge of the Order of the Knights of St. Catherine of Mount Sinai who were created in 1063 to protect pilgrims on their way to and from the Holy Sepulchre. It would therefore have been a most welcome sign on the road. Similarly the sign 'Cat and Fiddle' may have originally been 'Kit and Fiddle', 'Kit' being the diminutive form of Christopher, the patron saint of travellers, a sign which would also have attracted pilgrims and travellers. Alternatively 'Kit' may refer to the small form of a fiddle used by dancing-masters. The 'Cat and Fiddle' sign would then have advertised where music on the 'Kit and Fiddle' could be enjoyed. The Domesday Book records an inn by the name of 'Catherine la Fidèle' near the Saxon monastery at Christchurch, Twynham. There is still an inn on the same site which is now known as 'The Cat and Fiddle'.

Thus the cat which in Egypt had been a religious symbol as well as a pet and a practical asset, spread through Europe and became an established ingredient of medieval society. At first only of value to the farmer, it later became a subject of literature, riddles and proverbs, and featured on inn signs and in small carvings in churches. It was also recognized as a symbol for aspirations to liberty. We shall now see that Shakespeare's 'harmless necessary cat' continued to be remembered for religious associations which developed in Egypt but which also percolated into Europe.

3

Changing with the times

I am the cat of cats, I am
    The everlasting cat!
Cunning and old, and sleek as jam,
    The everlasting cat!
I hunt the vermin in the night—
    The everlasting cat!
For I see best without the light—
    The everlasting cat!
                    (WILLIAM BRIGHTY RANDS)

Although the Egyptians did not willingly allow their cats to leave the country there was no impediment to the flow of their religious ideas. The deities with whom the cat was linked and the religious beliefs they embodied were a strong influence beyond the borders of Egypt. Ideas as they develop or are transplanted tend to take their symbols with them and when ideas lose their dynamic force they stagnate and degenerate and the symbols associated with them are also debased. Both these processes happened to the cat. The Egyptian Cat-Goddesses were equated with Greek and Roman counterparts and the male cat Ra was adopted by the superstitious and credulous. But in both cases the new symbolic identifications enabled the cat to survive as a religious symbol— to become the 'everlasting cat'.

Naturally some Greeks were attracted to Egyptian religious practices and others criticized them. In the play called *The Cities* by Anaxandrides of Rhodes one of the characters says to an Egyptian:

'If you see a cat indisposed you weep for it,
For my part I am pleased to kill it for its skin'.

This was about 350 B.C. Thirty years later Timocles says that he certainly would not fear violating cat shrines when irreverence to the great gods themselves went unpunished. This suggests that some people in Greece worshipped the cat which might explain the significance of the cats represented on Greek coins and vase paintings.

Greek interest in Egyptian religion led them to see that many of their own deities were analogous to Egyptian ones. For instance, at Samos a bronze cat of Egyptian origin was dedicated to the Greek Goddess Hera. Although she herself had no connection with the cat it was realized that the Egyptian Goddess who corresponded to Hera was Mut from whom Bast and Sekhnet were derived.

The principal deities of the Graeco–Roman pantheon to which the cat became attached were: Venus and Aphrodite, Artemis and Diana, Demeter and Hecate. The reason for the identification is not always clear and we must remember that we are looking back in time over two thousand years during which period the worship of these goddesses totally collapsed. All that we can do is to point out the possible lines of thought and development which led to these identifications.

In the case of Venus and Aphrodite, which were respectively the Roman and Greek names for the same Love-Goddess, the obvious parallel was Bast. The Egyptians regarded her as a 'Goddess of Pleasure' epitomizing the ardour of animal passion, and her attributes and functions were later attached to Isis, a Mother and Fertility-Goddess. Artemis, the Virgin-Goddess of Hunting and Forests was a Greek agricultural deity with many duties. Her symbol was the moon and she presided over childbirth and protected the young. The Greeks therefore identified her with Isis. But Artemis could also be destructive and cause sickness and death. For this reason they associated her with Sekhnet, the destructive counterpart of Bast, and also with the old Egyptian Mother-Goddess, Mut. Still later Artemis was identified with Hecate who was originally a Moon-Goddess and became the Goddess of the Underworld. In this capacity Hecate survived into the Middle Ages. She was connected with enchantments and magic spells, and she haunted cross-roads, tombs and scenes of crime. On the eve of the full moon offerings were made to her image at cross-roads where according to tradition buried treasure belonging to her was guarded by cats.

In Roman mythology Diana corresponds to Artemis. Her ancient identification with the cat is attested by the Roman poet Ovid in his book the *Metamorphoses* which contains many tales based on what were already, in his time, old folk traditions. He recounts that when the gods had to flee from the giants they took on animal disguises and Diana transformed herself into a cat.

Stemming from these parallels which the Greeks and Romans drew between their goddesses and the Egyptian Cat-Goddesses, Mut, Bast and Sekhnet, and also the Goddess Isis who carried a sistrum with a cat decoration on it, there persisted in Europe, albeit through a series of gradual transformations, a belief that the cat was sacred to Venus, Diana, Hecate and Demeter. That these beliefs became ever more confused is partly because after Rome became Christian this complex of deities continued to exert their thrall but without the benefit of an educated priesthood and under increasing pressure from the rising tide of Christianity.

In this light it is interesting to speculate on the possible meaning of carvings of cats catching mice which occur on the Norman fonts at Hodnet, Salop and at Kilburn in Yorkshire. Also, in the museum of St. Germain-en-Laye in the north of France there is a stone altar sculptured with cats at which baptisms were celebrated at the end of the eleventh century. These cats carved on fonts or where baptisms were performed may hark back to a time when a goddess to whom the cat was sacred was the guardian of life and death. Kathleen Raine has pointed out that the Christian font symbolizes a spring or stream as the source of life. In Greek myth the spring flows from an inaccessible source and is guarded by women. The real significance of these carvings is probably now beyond discovery. All that we can say is that long after the old pagan goddesses had been forgotten in Europe the cat was still believed to have some effect upon the aspects of life that the goddesses had once presided over: love, death and disease, the fertility of the soil and the phases of the moon.

As Isis in one aspect was concerned with the fruitfulness of

Egyptian soil and great spring and autumn festivals were held in her honour, the Greeks saw that she corresponded to Demeter, their goddess of grain and crop growing. According to myth Osiris, the husband of Isis, showed the Egyptians the use of corn and his dismembered body had been scattered throughout Egypt. Another form of the same theme is the story of Persephone, the daughter of the Corn-Goddess Demeter, who spent half of each year in the underworld. As Ra, symbolized by the male cat, was later incorporated into Osiris it is not too surprising to find that until recent times in Europe there were harvest rituals involving a cat which seem to be derived from pagan cults of Demeter, Isis and Osiris. At the end of the year when the corn had been harvested and threshed, it would have seemed to the early farming communities as if all plant life was coming to an end and dying. In order to ensure that seeds would grow up again next year a human sacrifice was performed. The person so sacrificed represented 'The Corn Spirit' and his body or dismembered parts of it were either buried in the fields to ensure a good crop next year or thrown into the river to act as a rain charm.

Gradually this human sacrifice gave place either to a mock sacrifice or to an animal one. The animal sacrificed in different localities varied, but where the representative of the Corn Spirit was a cat the ceremonies involved either actually killing a cat or a cat being dressed up and honoured by the villagers. In some areas all that remains of the old rituals are harvest expressions using the word 'cat'.

Sir James Frazer in *The Golden Bough* tells us that around Amiens when the harvesting was about to be finished they said 'they are going to kill the cat' and when the last corn had been cut a cat was killed in the farmyard. In other parts of France a live cat was placed under the last bundle of corn to be threshed and was killed by a blow from the flails. The following Sunday this cat was roasted and eaten at the harvest feast. At Briancon in Dauphiné when reaping began a cat was decorated with ribbons, ears of corn and flowers. If one of the reapers accidentally cut himself the cat was made to lick the wound. When the reaping was finished it was again decorated and there was dancing and merriment. Afterwards the village girls solemnly stripped the cat of its finery. In Scotland a handful of reaped corn or straw laid on the ground was called 'a cat'.

French peasants used to describe the end of the harvest as 'killing' or 'catching the cat'. If the harvest was good, they said 'the cat is fat' but if 'the cat is lean' it had been a poor harvest. The man who cut the last handful of wheat was said to have 'caught the cat'. At Vesoul they said 'we have the cat by the tail' as harvesting finished. In Silesia the man who gave the last stroke to the threshing was called 'Tom Cat' and around Lyon the last sheaf and the harvest supper were both called 'The Cat'.

The peasants of Russia, Poland and Bohemia believed that to bury a cat alive in the cornfields would ensure a good crop. In Transylvania and Bohemia black tom-cats were killed and buried in the fields on Christmas Eve and at the sowing of the first seed, to prevent evil spirits from harming the crops. It was also customary to bury black cats under fruit trees to stimulate their growth. In the French Province of Bearn a kitten buried alive in the ground was believed to prevent weeds from growing.

Near Kiel the children were warned not to go into the corn-fields because it was said, 'the Cat sits there'. In the Eisenach Oberland they were told that 'the Corn Cat will come and fetch you'. Not unconnected with these threats is the custom at Grüneberg, Silesia, where the reaper who cut the last corn was called the 'Tom Cat' and was decorated with rye stalks and green withies and a long plaited tail was attached to his back. Sometimes he had a companion similarly decked out, who played the part of a female cat. Their role in the ceremonies was to run after the villagers and try to beat them with sticks. This buffoonery and the warnings to children were vestiges from the time when it was a necessary ritual for a human being to be caught and killed as a sacrifice to satisfy a harvest deity.

The male cat which symbolized Ra, the Egyptian Sun-God who fought with the forces of darkness, did not become attached to a Greek or a Roman deity. Instead his influence continued to be felt in folk-belief and superstition. The Egyptians are supposed to have believed that both the sun and the moon had an effect upon the cat's eyes and that the size of its pupils varied according to the height of the sun in the sky. This implied a symbolic and not an actual correspondence. It would be very natural for people whose idea of cause and effect was more a matter of sympathetic magic, to associate the mysterious waxing and waning of the moon with the curious ability of the cat to change the size of the pupils of its eyes. It will be remembered that Ra later became Osiris who was killed and became the 'King of the Dead' and that the cat on the top of Isis's sistrum was regarded as a symbol of the moon. Therefore Osiris and Isis, his wife, formed a sun–moon pair. Thus, in Egyptian thought the cat became associated with the sun for the Sun-God Ra, and with the moon through both Osiris, who succeeded Ra, and Isis.

After Egypt's power declined the reason for the identification of the cat with Ra, Osiris and Isis was forgotten and the meaning of their symbolic affinities was debased. It was now only vaguely remembered that the cat was associated with the worship of the sun and moon because of its eyes and gradually the emphasis changed and people believed that the cat's eyes possessed magical properties which could be used for occult purposes and for the cure of diseases of the eye. This is the explanation of the many superstitions found all over Europe which require a cat, or more specifically its eyes, for recipes to cure a sty or cast a spell to see evil spirits.

> Take the afterbirth of the first born black cat, which is the daughter of a first born black cat, burn it, grind it to powder and then put the ashes into your eyes.

This recipe, taken from the great compendium of Jewish law and legend known as the Talmud, is for use if one wishes to see the evil spirits: however its tone is early medieval, suggesting that it was a Christian borrowing from a debased or misunderstood Egyptian tradition which was incorporated into the Talmud when it was written down, rather than part of the authentic oral tradition. It is an example of the rules of sympathetic magic. A cat or a cat's head or specifically its eyes would have the magic power to affect 'seeing'. Folk-cures for eye complaints, some of them still in use, which involve the use of a cat or its parts, were probably originally derived from magical recipes of this sort.

A very common cure for a sty was to rub it with the tail of a black cat. A Cornish version has this spell to chant with it:

> Stroke the eye, from the nose out, with the tail of a black cat, saying with a stroke to each line: 'I poke thee, I don't poke thee, I toke the quell that's under the 'ee.
> Oh, qualyway. Oh, qualyway.'

Another remedy required only a single hair from the tip of a black cat's tail, but this had to be plucked when the new moon rose in a cloudless sky. The hair was then drawn across the eye nine times.

Not only folk-lore but naturalists such as Edward Topsell, who in 1607 wrote a *Historie of Foure-Footed Beastes*, subscribed to the view that a cat could cure diseases of the eye. He gave the following recipe:

> Take the head of a black cat, which hath not a spot of another colour in it, and burn it to powder in an earthen pot, leaded or glazed within; then take this powder, and through a quill, blow it thrice a day into thy eye; and if in the night any heat do thereby annoy thee, take two leaves of an oke, wet in cold water, and bind them to the eye, and so shall all pain flie away, and blindness depart, although it hath oppressed thee a whole year: and this medicine is approved by many physicians both elder and later.

A common belief in Scotland and the north of England was that when someone died all cats must be carefully shut up till after the funeral. Should one enter the room where the corpse was laid out, or leap over it, then the first person to meet that cat afterwards would be stricken with blindness. Similarly, in Eastern Europe it was thought that if a cat accidentally crossed a corpse before burial, the next person to meet it would become a vampire. Northumbrians would kill a cat if it crossed a corpse, and in this century an old woman whose job it was to lay out corpses, would on no account let a cat near a dead body as she said it would tear out and eat the eyes.

In Scotland the expression 'to cast the cat over him' is now used when someone is grossly exaggerating, but at one time a cat was literally passed over the body of a patient who was delirious with fever. In both cases the purpose of the cat is to make the person see things as they really are, whether he sees things as other than they are because of fever, or because he exaggerates.

The ancient Egyptian word *mau* for a cat meant also 'to see' and the idea has persisted that cats, which have exceptionally good visual powers, were also, on the basis of sympathetic magic, 'seers' in the occult sense. In medieval times the Scots resorted to the ritual burning of cats to obtain the gift of 'second sight' and an occult treatise called 'The Magnus or Celestial Intelligence' written by Francis Barrett at the beginning of the nineteenth century, claims:

> There are some collyriums which make us see the images of spirits in the air or elsewhere; which I can make of the gall of a man and the eyes of a black cat, and some other things.

Typical of books written for the credulous in all ages, the claim reminds us of the recipe for seeing evil spirits given in the Talmud. This line of magical thinking takes an interesting twist in a 'Thieving Magic' from South Slavonia collected by Sir James Frazer whereby the ashes of a blind cat can be used to prevent a person seeing that he is being robbed:

> To pilfer at market—burn a blind cat and throw a pinch of its ashes over the person to be stolen from.

Not only was the Egyptian intuition of the symbolic meaning of the cat's changing eyes misunderstood and debased into magic but later naturalists even attempted to find a causal connection between the size of the cat's pupils and the sun and the moon. Edward Topsell recorded as an Egyptian observation that the cat's eyes shone more fully at the full moon and were dimmer at the change and wane of the moon. The eyes of the male cat, he believed, also varied with the sun, the pupils being like slits when the sun rose and becoming round at midday.

Marc de Vulson who died in 1658 wrote that the cat's eyes

wax and wane in imitation of the moon; for as the moon, according as she shares in the light of the sun, changes her face every day, so is the cat moved by a similar affection toward the moon, its pupils waxing and waning at the times when that heavenly body is crescent or in its decline.

and another naturalist, William S. Salmon writing in 1693 said:

As to its Eyes, Authors say that they shine in the Night, and see better at the full, and more dimly at the change of the Moon; as also that the Cat doth vary his Eyes with the Sun, the Apple of its Eye being long at Sun rise, round towards Noon, and not to be seen at all at night, but the whole Eye shining in the night. These appearances of the Cat's Eyes I am sure are true, but whether they answer to the times of the day, I never observed.

Even in the nineteenth century a missionary could seriously report that some Chinese villagers had shown him how they used the cat's eyes to tell the time of day. 'They pointed out' he said:

that the pupil of their eyes went on constantly growing narrower until twelve o'clock, when they became like a fine line, as thin as a hair, drawn perpendicularly across the eye, and that after twelve the dilation recommenced.

When we had attentively examined the eyes of all the cats at our disposal, we concluded that it was past noon, as all the eyes perfectly agreed upon the point.

Whether in association with degenerate magical practices, or attached to Greek and Roman goddesses, the cat as a mystical symbol has shown a remarkable capacity for survival in Europe. Before tracing further its many and various transformations we will take one final look at Egypt and the Middle East to see how the cat fared there.

4

A lingering reverence

For he made a great figure in Egypt
for his signal services.
(CHRISTOPHER SMART)

What became of the cats that remained in Egypt and the belief in their divinity after the power of Egypt was broken? Religious ideas seldom disappear without leaving traces and in Egypt and the Middle East a general sympathy towards cats lingered on.

In the Gnostic work called 'Pistis Sophia' belonging to the Coptic Christians who were descendants of the Egyptians, the way in which the abodes of the soul after death are described shows that the cat and the snake were still thought of as symbols of the forces of light and darkness. Sir Ernest Budge gives a translation of it in his book *The Gods of the Egyptians*. Jesus is explaining to the Virgin Mary that:

> The outer darkness is a great serpent, the tail of which is in its mouth, and it is outside the whole world, and surroundeth the whole world; in it there are many places of punishment, and it containeth twelve halls wherein severe punishment is inflicted. In each hall is a governor, but the face of each governor differeth from that of his neighbour . . . and the governor of the second hall hath as his true face the face of a cat, and they call him in his place Kharakhar. . . . And in the eleventh hall there are many governors, and there are seven heads, each of them having as its true face the face of a cat, and the greatest of them, who is over them, they call in his place Rhôkhar. . . . These twelve governors are in the serpent of outer darkness, and each of them hath a name according to

49

the hour, and each of them changeth his face according to the hour.

This is interpreted to mean that the forces of good and evil are in a balanced harmony to execute the will of God who in the first centuries A.D. was probably still thought of by the Copts as Ra or Osiris.

The *Gospel of the Holy Twelve* is a document of a quite different level of authenticity from 'Pistis Sophia'. Its contents were received in visions which the Reverend G. J. Ousley wrote down for publication in 1923. He claims it to be a translation of an early Christian document preserved in one of the Buddhist monasteries in Tibet, where it was hidden by some of the Essene community from the hands of corrupters. About the birth of Jesus in a cave it says:

... there were in the same cave an ox, and a horse, and an ass, and a sheep, and beneath the manger was a cat with her little ones ...

Another legend in it tells that Jesus saw some men tormenting a cat and commanded them to stop. They abused him and would not desist so he made a whip and drove them off. According to this source Jesus is also supposed to have protected a young stray cat, picking it up and carrying it in his robe. Later he fed it and gave it to one of his followers who was a widow.

Even after a lapse of nearly two thousand years, Lady Duff-Gordon who lived in Egypt in the 1880s could report an occurrence which explained the Egyptian's horror at the idea of killing a cat and revealed that traces of reverence for it still lingered. She was sitting drinking tea with a group of Egyptians when a cat walked into the room. She put down a saucer of milk for it but it ran away. One of the men then said that she did right to offer it milk because one should always be kind to cats since they got very little to eat at home. This particular cat, he explained, was really the butcher boy, who was a twin. He went on to tell her of the belief that all twins who have to go to bed hungry go out foraging at night in the form of cats. Their bodies lie in their beds as if dead and if anyone disturbs them they die. People were not afraid of these humans in cat form because they only wanted food. On enquiry she found this was a common belief among both Coptic Christians and Muslims in Egypt.

The Jews in the Middle East would have been well aware that their neighbours and one-time captors, the Egyptians, reverenced the cat. They would have regarded the many statues and paintings of cat-headed gods and goddesses, and the live cats kept in religious sanctuaries, as idolatrous. It is interesting that rats and mice were not among the plagues inflicted upon Egypt in the days of Moses, perhaps because it was thought that they would be quickly dealt with by their feline deities. So it is not surprising that there are no biblical references to cats except in the Apocrypha. In the Epistle of Jeremiah, supposedly a letter written to the Jews in slavery at Babylon but probably not composed before the first century B.C. there is an exhortation against being tempted to worship the Babylonian idols which could not possibly be efficacious when they were not even properly looked after by their priests:

> . . . and when vermin from the ground devour them [the idols] and their clothing, they do not perceive it; their faces are blackened by the smoke from the temple. Bats, swallows, and birds light on their bodies and on their heads; so do cats also. Therefore you may be sure they are not gods, so you must not stand in awe of them.

It is now uncertain whether these were really cats. The word which was translated as 'cats' some experts say should read 'wagtails'. On the other hand if the translation should really read 'cats' they may have been sacred ones, not strays. The Babylonians believed that when a human being who had attained to a certain degree of holiness died, a cat acted as host to his soul for the rest of its natural life. Then when the cat died the soul of the holy-man would go to heaven with it. However, when they saw a black cat, which was regarded as an evil omen, they cried *Hilka Bescha* meaning 'Be off, accursed one'.

Among the Spanish Jews a folk-tale tells that the first wife of Adam was Lilith, but she refused to obey him and flew away as a vampire. In the Book of Isaiah, Lilith is referred to as a screech-owl which, like the cat, is an animal that hunts at night. According to the Jewish folk-tale Lilith still lives and assumes the shape of a huge black cat named 'El Broosha'. In this form she seizes new-born babies to suck their blood. Here could be the origin of the widespread European belief that a cat can 'suck the breath out of' or suffocate a sleeping child and that black cats in particular are dangerous to sleeping babies.

It seems that any appreciation of the cat as a religious symbol which Christians might have inherited from Egypt was more than counterbalanced by feelings stemming from Jewish experiences in Babylon and Egypt which equated the cat with idolatry and so made it evil.

Quite different from the Jewish or Christian attitude was that of the Muslim world which treated cats with great affection. The Baghdad poet Ibn Alalaf Ahnaharwany who died about A.D. 930 wrote ruefully of his cat who was killed for hunting pigeons in a dove-cote. The theme of the poem is said to be taken from an Indian tale but it also has the ring of personal experience with a particular pet cat:

> *Poor Puss is gone! 'Tis fate's decree—*
> *Yet I must still her loss deplore,*
> *For dearer than a child was she,*
> *And ne'er shall I behold her more.*
>
> *With many a sad presaging tear*
> *This morn I saw her steal away,*
> *While she went on without a fear*
> *Except that she should miss her prey.*
>
> *I saw her to the dove-house climb,*
> *With cautious feet and slow she stept,*
> *Resolving to balance loss of time*
> *By eating faster than she crept.*
>
> *Her subtle foes were on the watch*
> *And mark'd her course, with fury fraught,*
> *And while she hoped the birds to catch,*
> *An arrow's point the huntress caught.*

In fancy she had got them all,
And drunk their blood, and suck'd their breath;
Alas! she only got a fall,
And only drank the draught of death.

Why, why was pigeon's flesh so nice,
That thoughtless cats should love it thus?
Had'st thou but lived on rats and mice,
Thou had'st been living still, poor Puss.

Curst be the taste, howe'er refined,
That prompts us for such joys to wish,
And curst the dainty where we find
Destruction lurking in the dish.

When Sultan El-Daher-Beybars, who reigned in Egypt and Syria about 1260, died he bequeathed an orchard near Cairo to benefit cats. The proceeds from the sale of the fruit were to be used to buy food for stray and hungry ones. Towards the end of the nineteenth century in Cairo it was still possible to dispose of unwanted cats by taking them to several points in the city where funds were provided to feed them every afternoon.

However, in the *Arabian Nights* Jinn or Jinneee appear to mankind as serpents, dogs, cats or human beings. Unlike angels they may be good or bad. One of the stories, 'The Porter and the Ladies of Baghdad', tells of a young man who was enchanted and turned into an ape by an evil Jinnee. But a Princess who was in love with the young man possessed greater ability as an enchantress than the Jinnee. In the process of freeing the young man from his enchantment, she and the Jinnee go through a series of animal transformations in the course of which the Jinnee at one stage becomes a black cat.

A curious tale was told to the nineteenth-century traveller, Edward Lane, by an aged sheik who once owned a black cat. The sheik had been awakened by knocking at midnight and over-heard his cat talking with a Jinnee. The Jinnee wanted to come into the sheik's house to eat and drink, but the cat said that the lock on the door, the bread basket and the water jar had all been secured by having the name of Allah pronounced over them. He suggested that the Jinnee should go next door and then went with him to let him into the neighbour's house. The next morning the sheik gave the cat a much larger breakfast than usual and said 'O my cat, thou knowest that I am a poor man: bring to me then a little gold'; upon which words the cat immediately disappeared, and he saw it no more.

A variant of the Noah's Ark story traditionally believed to have been told by Muhammad occurs in an early Muslim book. It tells how when the Ark was loaded some of his followers complained that the rats would eat their stores. 'God therefore caused the lion to sneeze, when there came forth from it the cat: the rat then concealed itself from the view of the cat.'

The Prophet is always described as being very fond of cats. 'Cats are not impure, they keep watch around us' is a saying ascribed to him by one of his followers. It is said that he preached holding a cat in his arms, that he used water from which a cat had drunk for his purifications and that his wife ate from a dish that a cat had eaten from. When he wanted to honour his faithful follower Abd-er-rahim, he gave him the title of 'Abuhareira' which means 'Father of the Cat'.

> *Here purrs Abuhareira's cat*
> *Round him with coaxing bland;*
> *A holy creature sure is that*
> *Stroked by the Prophet's hand.*

So wrote Goethe in celebration of Abd-er-rahim's title and the now famous story of Muhammad's own cat 'Muezza'. One day when she was asleep on the sleeve of his robe he was called away on business. Rather than disturb his cat he cut off his sleeve. On his return Muezza got up and bowed to him in thanks. The Prophet then stroked her three times down the length of her back. This, it is believed, conferred upon cats the ability to land on their feet if they fell from a height. In modern Turkey tabby cats with four stripes between their ears are called 'Holy Cats' because, it is said, the four stripes show where the Prophet stroked Muezza. To this day cats are allowed in mosques and are not molested because they were Muhammad's favourite animal.

The reason given for Muhammad's fondness for cats was that one day a snake crawled into his sleeve for warmth. When the Prophet asked it to get out, it refused. 'Very well,' he said, 'let us refer the matter to the cat.' To this the snake agreed. The cat then said to the snake: 'Put out your head so that we may better discuss this matter.' No sooner did the snake do so than the cat pounced and carried it off. Therefore, concludes the story, 'no cat should ever be struck with anything except a cotton ball'. This story is almost certainly not the basis for the Prophet's love of cats, but a tale told later to explain it. Could the tale reflect the story of Ra and the Serpent enacted on a more domestic scale? There is, however, the Arab proverb which says:

A cat bitten once by a snake dreads even rope

which demonstrates that even if the Muslims remembered that a mythical cat could deal with a mythical snake, they knew very well that a real cat could be very scared by one. Indeed, in the Arab world there must have existed a sympathetic attitude towards cats long before Muslim times. Two or three cats usually accompany the caravan which takes the Sacred Carpet from Cairo to Mecca and an eyewitness account written in 1835 of a religious procession which took place at the time of the covering of the Kaaba (the black stone within the Great Mosque at Mecca which is the object of Muslim pilgrimage) says that the pageant included several tall camels lightly dyed with red henna, and with highly-decorated saddles. Boys and girls rode upon them, and on some there were several cats. One wonders whether the cats were included in the procession because of the Prophet's known liking for them or whether it was a reference to some older custom.

In ancient times, before the coming of Islam, the Arabs in Persia worshipped a Golden Cat and the word *gatu* for a cat occurs in Zend, the language of the Zoroastrians. Thus the Arabs have known cats from the time of their first contact with the Persians. At least one ancient custom remains from these times. Members of the Muslim mystic brotherhood of Siddi Heddi entice stray cats into their sanctuaries, fatten them up, and once a year eat them during a ritual feast. This is in spite of the fact that

Islam forbids the eating of all animals which are themselves flesh-eaters.

Perhaps it was a knowledge of customs such as these practised by their enemies, which led the Knights Templar into bad habits. Originating as a knightly order recruited with the purpose of raising funds for the Crusades, they developed into a ruthless military and political body who became the bankers of the Eastern Mediterranean. When they became too powerful they were persecuted and exterminated on a variety of unpleasant charges including worshipping cats.

There is no truth however in the tradition that cats were brought to Western Europe by returning Crusaders. They had spread throughout Europe long before. The only cat introduced at this time was the Persian which is first mentioned in the *Romance of the Rose* written in France in the thirteenth century. This does not exclude the possibility that stories and cult practices involving cats, such as those supposedly practised by the Knights Templar, seeped into Western Europe in more or less garbled form as a result of the Crusades and the long period of Muslim harassment to which Mediterranean countries were subjected. But it is likely that these contacts only served to strengthen beliefs and customs that were already widespread.

5

The World Serpent

I know of course the cat's origin—the incubation
of 'greybeard'
The cat was gotten on a stove—has a girl's
nose, a hare's head,
A tail of snake's venom, claws of a viper,
Feet of cloudberries, the rest of its body
is of the wolf's race.

(*A Magic Song of the Finns*)

To the Egyptian both the coiled snake and the curled-up cat symbolized eternity, and in Scandinavia too the cat and the serpent formed a mythic unity. The old Norse Sagas seem a far cry from the cults of Egypt, yet it has been shown that the belief in the soul making a journey by boat after death spread from Egypt to Northern Europe and Scandinavia along the old Amber Trade Route which distributed amber from the coast of Jutland and the Baltic to Greece, and which was already well established by the second millennium B.C. If funeral practices could spread in this way, why not beliefs about cats? With this in mind it is interesting to examine some of the old stories and traditions of Scandinavia and to see the influence they have had upon customs and superstitions which connect the cat with storms at sea.

The Norse Sagas tell of a 'World Serpent' who sometimes appeared in the guise of a cat. Preserved in them is the story that on one occasion Thor, who was immensely strong, went with his friend Loki to visit the land of the giants. He was invited by the giants to compete in various trials of strength, all of which he failed miserably. At last they asked derisively if he would like to try picking up the old grey cat. Thor, furious, grasped it round the middle, but however hard he heaved he could only raise one of its paws from the floor. Later, the giants told him it was no ordinary cat but Midgard, the World Serpent which lies at the bottom of the sea, encircling the earth. They had all been terrified when Thor's strength had proved great enough to raise it a little way from the depths of the ocean. At another time Thor went fishing and caught this great serpent. A terrible tussle ensued, Thor raising the serpent up so far that his companion in the boat saw its head and, panic-stricken, cut the line.

Thor's friend Loki was the son of a giant, handsome but perverse. Always scheming, he sometimes helped and sometimes obstructed the other gods. He had fathered the monstrous wolf, Fenrir, which grew so large and menacing that the gods wanted it fastened up but could find no chain strong enough to hold it. Finally, the dwarfs forged a magic chain made of the impalpable and secret things of the world. One of these was the noise of a cat's footfall.

Early Christian church carving in Scandinavia, some of which is still preserved in the beautiful old stave churches, makes great use of the snake motif in decoration. This is said to be because the convulsions of Midgard, the World Serpent, signified the end of the pagan world. It is extremely interesting that at Vågå the west front of the old Norwegian stave church shows carvings of animals which are described as having 'short, rounded, cat-like heads'. On one column the animals have long tails and are covered with a scaly skin like that of a viper. Is this, as it has been suggested, the Christian Lion of Judah fighting the pagan serpent, or does it represent the old snake-cat identification?

On the Atlantic seaboard of Europe and especially in Great Britain and Ireland there are many beliefs about cats and their influence upon the sea. Fishermen regard cats superstitiously and in the days when witches' powers were uncontested it was believed that storms could be aroused by throwing a cat into the sea. Are these traditions in some way connected with the old Norse tale of the great serpent of the ocean disguised as a cat that Thor was challenged to lift from the floor? Certainly one would expect that any disrespect shown to the cat would raise the ire of the World Serpent.

The World Serpent

Inhabitants of the Inner Hebrides tell the story of Thor's struggle with the cat in less awe-inspiring terms. The World Serpent was disguised as a beautiful white cat in the home of the giants. Thor, who liked cats, made friendly advances to it. 'The cat-worm opened one eye and smiled politely' says the tale, but when Thor bent to pick it up it was all his strength could do to raise its forepaws from the ground. The giants crowded round begging him to stop and telling him that the cat was really Midgard with the weight of the world encircled in it. Had he lifted the cat the world of men might have ended. So Thor was persuaded to leave the cat alone. But he could not help wondering if he was strong enough to lift the serpent from its home in the deep of the ocean. The tale then goes on to recount the adventure of Thor's fishing trip.

It is curious that in many parts of Europe one can still find sayings which appear to reflect a vague memory or awareness of an identity between cats and snakes, as for instance in the proverb from Brittany which says:

The tongue of a cat is poison, the tongue of the dog cures.

Cats seem to have been thought of as less fearful aspects of snakes and Lady Gregory who in the late nineteenth and early twentieth centuries devoted herself to collecting the folk-tales and beliefs of the peasantry in the West of Ireland found that they believed cats had actually changed from serpents into cats at some stage in the earth's history:

Cats were serpents, and they were made into cats at the time, I suppose, of some change in the world. That's why they're hard to kill and why it's dangerous to meddle with them. If you annoy a cat it might claw you or bite you in a way that would put poison in you, and that would be the serpent's tooth.

When the naturalist Edward Topsell was writing in the early seventeenth century it was thought that a cat could cure itself if bitten by a snake:

. . . Some have said that Cats will fight with Serpents, and Toads, and kill them, and perceiving that she is hurt by them;

she presently drinketh water and is cured: but I cannot consent unto this opinion: it being true of the Weasell as shall be afterwards declared.

Although Topsell did not agree, he thought that perhaps weasels could. This we shall see later is a very interesting distinction. Strange too is the medieval medical report of monks becoming ill as a result of playing with a cat because, it was said, the cat had previously been playing with a serpent whose poison had been mysteriously transferred to the cat without making the cat itself ill.

Fishermen on both sides of the North Sea are still superstitious about cats. Near Peterhead nobody mentions a cat while baiting a line, and no crew-member of a Dieppe fishing boat would dare to talk about cats while at sea. On the other hand, round Scarborough black cats are regarded as lucky by fishermen's wives, who keep them in the belief that they have the power to ensure their husbands' safe return from the sea.

The *International Maritime Dictionary* lists no fewer than twenty-two nautical terms using the word 'cat'. Fifteen of these are terms associated with the anchor and its tackle or with the process of raising and lowering the anchor. Here are some examples:

Catting the anchor: Hauling the ring of the anchor to the cathead.

Cathead: A beam of wood or metal projecting on either side of the bow to support the raised anchor clear of the bow. In former days the ends of the cathead were carved to represent the head of a cat.

Cat-hook: A large hook used to lift the anchor to the cathead.

Cat-back: A small line bent into the cat-hook to turn the cat-hook as required in catting the anchor.

Cat-fall: The rope hauled upon to hoist the anchor to the cathead.

Do these terms refer to the cat-serpent at the bottom of the sea? One can quite easily imagine the fearful sailor feeling that the anchor he hauled up from the depth had been in the vicinity of Thor's World Serpent and might bring that terrible monster up with it. He might even be accused of imitating Thor and fishing for the serpent with the anchor hook. It would have been prudent to attempt to avoid danger by naming everything concerned with the anchor in honour of the serpent but using the name of his safer, less terrible form, the cat.

A story from the Inner Hebrides of a man out fishing who thinks he is being 'called' by the Devil, contains the wonderfully eerie description . . .

. . . when suddenly the sea went still, still as a cat and it watching.

This and the expression 'cat's paw' for a faint breeze which just ripples the sea suggest that the cat is intimately concerned with the condition of the sea. When the ship's cat is more than usually playful sailors say 'The cat has a gale of wind in her tail' which means an approaching storm. The Scots say the cat is 'raising wind' if it scratches the table or chair legs.

The story of the 'Four-Eyed Cat' connects ships, storms, witches and cats. It was collected by the folk-lorist Ruth Tongue in 1955 from the twelve-year-old daughter of a lightship sailor from Harwich and Dovercourt in Essex who heard it from her grandparents:

There was a gentleman had a beautiful daughter who was bad at heart, and they said she knew more than a Christian should, and they wanted to swim her, but no one dared because of her father. She drew a spell on a poor fisherman, and he followed for love of her wherever she went. He deserted his troth-plight maid, though he was to be married in a week, and he ran away to sea with the gentleman's daughter and unbeknown to all the rest (that is, the rest of the fleet) took her out with them to the fishing. She did it to spite her father's pride, but he thought himself well rid of her.

A storm blew up and the whole fishing fleet were lost to a man for they had on board a woman with them at sea, though none knew it but her lover. It was she that had whistled up the storm that had drowned her own lover, for she hated everyone. She was turned into a 'four-eyed cat', and ever after she haunted the fishing fleet. So that is why even now fishermen won't cast their nets before half-past three (cock-crow)—my uncles won't—and they always throw a bit back into the sea for the cat.

The reference to 'cock-crow' is because such a magic creature as a 'four-eyed cat' would be sure to have associations with the fairies and they must all be gone away at first cock-crow.

Old traditions name the Inner Hebridean island of Raasay as a great centre for witchcraft in the seventeenth century. In those days it was common practice for aristocratic families to place their children with foster-mothers for the first two years of their lives. Because there were so many witches on Raasay, the family who were the lords of the island, thinking to avoid the danger of their son and heir, Iain Garbh, being fostered out to one, sent him to a foster-mother on the Isle of Skye. Unfortunately they did not realize that she too was a witch. When Iain inherited Raasay he tried to stamp out witchcraft on the island. For a few years he succeeded in suppressing it but in the end the witches avenged themselves. They drowned him when he was sailing from Raasay to Skye. As his boat sailed through calm waters there came swimming a host of little black cats led by one large black one. She climbed the rigging and the others followed. The boat heeled over and all on board, except the cats, were drowned.

Another version of this tale says it was actually his foster-mother, a very strong witch, who drowned him. She and several other powerful witches raised a violent storm when he was sailing on a clear day. Over the ship hovered three ravens and soon twenty more arrived. They flew onto the boat and once there some turned into cats and some into frogs which he was known especially to dislike. They jumped all over the boat and even onto him so that it seemed as if all the witches of Scotland were there.

He guessed that the frogs were witches and drew his sword and slashed at the largest, saying 'What the big brindled one [the Devil] brought you here?' As soon as he swore, the Devil had power over him and caused him to strike with his sword so hard that the boat was cut in two. So Iain Garbh and his ship sank together. Everyone knew this story was true because a man taking shelter from a thunderstorm in a ruined hut on the nearby island of Uist, met with a large, black and very wet cat. He was about to kill it as a poaching cat when it turned into a local woman he knew. He asked what she was doing in cat-form and she replied that she had just come from the drowning of Iain Garbh.

Witches in the Highlands of Scotland could raise a storm and threaten ships at sea by drawing a cat through a fire or by throwing a cat into the sea. When James VI of Scotland and his Danish wife, Ann, were on a visit to Denmark between 1589 and 1590 so many storms arose that at one time boats were unable to cross the North Sea. Subsequently a group of people believed to be a coven of witches were tried for conspiring to cause a storm at sea by means of witchcraft. It was stated at the trial that at Leith, Scotland, they took a cat, christened it and bound parts of a dead man to it. Then at night, to the accompaniment of incantations by the whole coven, the cat was flung into the sea. 'Then arose the worst storm ever seen.' Another, more cynical account says the first cat swam ashore and a second one had to be thrown out.

Shakespeare's three witches in *Macbeth* were adept at raising storms. One of them was named 'Graymalkin', which was the name for a witch's cat. It was formed from a combination of the words 'gray' and 'Malkin', which latter is an obsolete diminutive form of Matilda or Maud, names that were sometimes used by themselves to mean a cat. Annoyed with a sailor's wife who will not share her chestnuts, the three witches conspire to shipwreck her husband.

Second Witch: I'll give thee a wind.
First Witch: Thou'rt kind.
Third Witch: And I another.

First Witch:	I myself have all the other;
	And the very ports they blow,
	All the quarters that they know
	I' the shipman's card.

. . .

	Though his bark cannot be lost,
	Yet it shall be tempest-tost.
	Look what I have.
Second Witch:	Show me, show me.
First Witch:	Here I have a pilot's thumb,
	Wrack'd as homeward he did come.

(*Macbeth*, *Act I, Sc. III*)

There is a curious description in a book of late Roman times by Pomponius Mela called *The Nine Priestesses of the Isle of Sark, situated in the British Sea.* He tells us that Sark was renowned for its 'Oracles of the God of the Galles' whose nine priestesses were vowed to eternal virginity. They could raise seas and winds, transform themselves into animals, heal disease and prophesy the future. They sound very much like the predecessors of witches and it is interesting to compare them with the people known as the Telchini of Rhodes who were said to have forged Neptune's trident and rode on seahorses in the armies of Dionysus. They had the evil eye, could assume animal form and cause hail, rain and snow. One source says they quit Rhodes after foretelling a great flood and another account states that they were driven out by Apollo. In either case they left Rhodes and wandered away presumably to found sanctuaries in other places, one of which may have been Sark.

Long after witches' powers had declined, the belief that a cat could influence the weather at sea continued to be held. When Henry Fielding was on a voyage to Lisbon in 1754 a kitten fell overboard. The captain gave orders to turn about, the sails were slackened and the boatswain stripped off and dived in. He managed to find the kitten and swam back to the ship, carrying it in his mouth. After lying on the deck in the sun for some time, it revived. Some of the sailors were disappointed at this because they said a drowned cat was the surest way to raise a favourable wind. On the other hand, it is obvious that at least the captain thought it was lucky to keep a cat on board. In Sicily if a cat began miaowing while the Rosary was being recited for sailors about to embark, it foretold a 'tedious' voyage but it is not clear whether 'tedious' meant lack of wind or too much of it.

Nineteenth-century superstitious attitudes to the luckiness or otherwise of cats at sea is illustrated by an episode which occurred during the Spanish American War of 1898. Instructions had been given by a U.S. salvage expert named Hobson to tow a Spanish wreck, which still had its cat aboard, to Charleston. A storm arose in the Gulf of Mexico which threatened to sink the wreck and drag down the tow ship. Unable to reach the cat, the Americans cut the tow rope and left cat and ship to sink together. Later, when it was discovered that the ship had drifted onto a reef in the Bahamas, Hobson, who had developed a liking for the cat, set out with the captain of the tow ship to recover it. They found that it had been adopted by the islanders and had to buy it back for a ridiculously high price. When they set sail again a storm arose which the captain was sure was due to the presence of the cat. In his view she had been responsible for the original disaster to the Spanish ship and two storms since. 'Not so' said the salvage expert; she had clung to her ship with exemplary fidelity and the island to which it had drifted was called 'Cat Island'. The account ends with Hobson and his cat sitting on the top deck, eating apple pie and watching the moon as the barometer rises.

A belief in the ability of the cat to forecast the weather may be the last, most attenuated form of belief in its power to raise storms at sea in the name of the World Serpent. It is widely believed that if the cat washes behind its ears it will rain. Herrick in the seventeenth century assumed this to be true when he wrote:

> *True Calenders, as Pusses eare*
> *Washt o're, to tell what change is neare.*

Before the Cambridgeshire fens were drained, cats were indispensable for forecasting floods. Every home, no matter how poor, had at least one. Several days before the rains came the cat would try to get upstairs to sleep. If it was prevented from doing this, it would choose a spot on top of the highest cupboard it could find. Thus were the family forewarned of impending high water and could take precautions in plenty of time. Cats were so well thought of that on Sunday they used to accompany the family to church or chapel and wait outside during the service. Afterwards they were taken for a short after-church stroll which was known as 'the cat's walk'. Perhaps this was to keep on the right side of them in case a cat could produce wet weather as well as forecast it.

In the fens it was also believed that if the cat left a sunny corner to sleep in the barn, or slept with its head tucked well round between its paws, rain was coming. It would be cold if the cat slept with all four paws tucked under its body, and warm if it slept stretched at full length. If it slept with its front paws covering its nose gusty, windy weather could be expected. The cat's whiskers were also good weather indicators. If they drooped it would rain, but if they stood out stiff fine weather could be relied on for a day or two.

In Ireland and Holland, and doubtless in other places too, it is still said that those who dislike cats will be carried to the cemetery in rain, and that those who mistreat them will have umbrellas at their weddings.

Contrary to expectation, the expression 'raining cats and dogs' is not connected with these beliefs. It is an English misunderstanding of the French expression that it is raining like a *catedupe*, which is a waterfall.

6

Of love and death

> Then came dark-bearded-Niord, and after
> him Freyia, thin robed, about her ankles slim
> The grey cats playing.
>
> (WILLIAM MORRIS)

In Northern Europe the Goddess Freya was an erotic figure in whose cult cats played a part. Described as riding in a cart drawn by two cats, she is said to have behaved in a thoroughly wanton manner, going out at night to satisfy her lust and having love affairs with most of the gods. This conspicuous erotic behaviour is very cat-like and as in the case of the World Serpent seems to reveal connections with Egypt where the Cat-Goddess Bast was regarded as having qualities which every woman wished to emulate. Iceland is a long way from Egypt but there, women who had been declared criminals were sewn into a sack with a cat and thrown into a pond known as 'The Drowning Pool'. This custom strongly recalls the ancient Egyptian custom of sewing an adulteress into a sack with a cat and throwing her into the Nile.

Other links with Egypt are provided from Finland where it was believed that the soul was led by a cat through hell to paradise. This reminds us that Bast and Isis led souls to Osiris, the King of the Dead, and that in Babylon the soul of a holy-man was taken to heaven by a cat. In the *Kalevala*, a heroic poem composed in the nineteenth century by the Finnish scholar Lönnrot but based on old Finnish folk songs and stories, it is related that one day a witch entered a house which was full of people and began to sing incantations. Within minutes everyone was thrown onto a sleigh drawn by a huge cat and carried off to Pohjola on the borders of Finland where there is perpetual night and evil spirits abound.

Freya's devotees were principally women who were sooth-sayers and seers. Cats were among the animal spirits that would help transport them on supernatural journeys which they took while in a state of trance. In an account from Greenland we learn that the women who practised Freya's cult wore gloves of white cat-skin with the fur on the inside.

It is possible that evidence of her cult is provided by the carvings found in the Oseberg burial-ground in Norway which dates from the late eighth or early ninth century A.D. It contains sleighs and a cart and opinion is divided as to the interpretation of the animal heads which decorate the corner posts of the sleighs. Some are quite cat-like, and some experts say they are intended to be lions carved by artists who had never seen any but had seen Carolingian carvings of them. One authority, Peter Anker, says the realistic feline characteristics of the rounded skull, small ears and short snouts are unmistakably cats:

> . . . one might have sufficient confidence in the artist's skill as to assume that he could carve an animal from his own world of experience and imagination—a cat or a lynx, for example. (One might even suggest the idea of the goddess Freyja's beasts, the cats who drew her wagon.)

It is tempting to suggest that the carvings of cats were intended to invoke images of Freya's cats but this argument is weakened by the fact that the cat-heads, if such they are, occur on one of the sleighs and not on the cart.

Originally Freya had been an Earth-Mother Goddess who both gave and took life. She was lover, mother and destroyer and in these three aspects she is still remembered in the many super-stitions which link the cat as Freya's symbol with death and disease as well as with love and marriage. As time went on Freya came to represent only the lover and destroyer aspects of the ancient Earth-Mother. The Mother part of the trinity continued under the name of the Goddess Frigg. Because they are in fact different aspects of the same unity, Frigg and Freya became con-fused and compounded in popular thought and Freya's special symbol, the cat, was attached to Frigg.

Sailors regard it as bad luck to set out upon a voyage on a Friday, the day sacred to Frigg. They also treat the cat with superstitious mistrust and a woman, especially a pregnant one, is regarded as dangerous on board ship. Adding these beliefs together it is apparent that sailors felt it was dangerous when embarking upon the sea, symbolic of the mystic waters in which life itself is created, either to leave port on Frigg's day or to take with them other symbols of the Goddess of Fertility such as a woman (especially if pregnant), or a cat. Loaded with symbols of Freya and Frigg they would be invoking too close an association with them which could be extremely dangerous for ordinary mortal men.

Freya in her role of lover was a blesser of love and marriage. Many superstitions and customs hark back to a time when she and her symbol the cat were the guardians of those about to marry. In French folk-lore a strange white cat miaowing on the doorstep foretells a speedy marriage and an English proverb says that whoever cares for cats will marry happily. Conversely, if a single girl accidentally treads on a cat's tail she will not marry that year. Another English proverb states that:

> *Whenever the cat of the house is black,*
> *The lasses of lovers will have no lack.*

In the English Midlands to receive a black cat as a wedding present brings good luck to the bride and she will also be lucky if a cat sneezes in her hearing either on the wedding day or the day before. Be it noted however that the expression to live under the 'sign of the cat's foot' means to be henpecked.

Among the Ozarks of Tennessee and Arkansas when a girl received a proposal of marriage and was uncertain whether to accept, she took three hairs from a cat's tail and folded them in a paper which she placed under the doorstep. Next morning she carefully unfolded the paper to see if the three hairs had formed themselves into a Y or an N, and replied to her suitor accordingly. These descendants of the Scots and Irish who left their homelands in the seventeenth century, preserved many customs and beliefs that were forgotten elsewhere. They said that to keep a black cat in the home meant that all the daughters in the family would remain spinsters, but in the south of England to have a black cat in the home ensured that all the daughters of the family would marry.

It is possible to surmise that where it is believed that a black cat will ensure the daughters' marriage, the cat is acting as a lucky charm of Freya. Where the black cat ensures that the daughters remain spinsters the source of the underlying rationale may go back further to a time when Freya's priestesses had been virgins like the Nine Priestesses of Sark. Since these superstitions are derived from beliefs passed on by oral tradition from generation to generation through simple peasant families it is not really surprising that the passage of time and geographical separation has led to apparent contradictions. It is now only possible to say that *a* belief once existed. Precisely what it was we shall never know.

The following Huntingdonshire proverb about kittens born in the month of May is derived from beliefs about the more wanton aspect of Freya and her cats:

May chets
Bad luck begets
And sure to make dirty cats.

In Celtic areas and to a lesser extent in other parts of Europe there is a curious belief that kittens born in the month of May should not be reared because, it is said, they are always dirty. In antiquity, May was the month when all over Europe people abstained from sexual intercourse in order to purify themselves in preparation for the great midsummer celebrations held in June. In Welsh mythology the hawthorn, whose flower is commonly known as 'may', symbolized the giant who will not let his daughter marry. The giant lived in a castle guarded by nine porters and nine watchdogs. The strength of the guard served to emphasize the strength of the taboo against marrying in May. It is still considered unlucky to marry in this month, which accounts for the popularity of April and June for weddings. Thus, as symbols of the erotic Freya, kittens born in May, the month of abstention, would have been ritually unclean and it would have been necessary to destroy them.

The Welsh giant who lived in a castle guarded by nine porters and nine watchdogs brings us to the mysterious number nine and the cat's proverbial nine lives. Snorri Sturluson, the Icelandic Saga writer, tells in the *Edda* how Odin gave Freya power over the nine worlds or, according to another version, the ninth world, which took nine nights riding through gloomy valleys to reach and which was entered by crossing a river by a golden bridge. The Welsh giant may be taken as a male replacement for an older earth-mother goddess, such as Freya, in order to bring the myth into line with the then new ideas of patriarchy.

As recounted earlier there were nine priestesses of Sark who could control the weather. They were probably one of the sources from which the later witches drew their lore, an example of which is a ritual described at a witch trial where it was said that a cat was drawn nine times through an iron gate to make a spell. 'Two-legged cats with thrice-nine lives' is a line in a litany to protect against witches. The magical power of drawing a hair of a cat's tail nine times across the eye to cure a sty has already been noted and the Egyptians, from whom the belief derived, also believed that the universe had been created by nine primal gods. Therefore there was an awareness, drawn from various sources, of a time when the cat was associated with the powers of creativity and the old earth-mother or fertility goddesses. As we have seen, these ancient goddesses, of which Freya was one, had three aspects: lover, mother and destroyer. Nine, being three-times-three, represented in religious thought a sort of holy of holies whose potency was widely recognized. Belief in the cat's nine lives must have developed because it was sacred to a goddess with three aspects for whom the number nine had ritual significance. Long after this lost its mystic force the cat's association with nine remained.

Like Bast's destructive counterpart, Sekhnet, and Isis who took souls to the Kingdom of the Dead, Freya's third aspect was destructive. We have already seen that in Egypt the sensuous Bast was linked with the lion-headed Sekhnet, the Goddess of

War and Sickness. Artemis, and Diana her Roman counterpart who, it was said, assumed cat-form on one occasion, could protect or destroy. Similarly Freya was the Goddess of War and Death as well as of Love. As foremost of the Valkyries, who were fierce female spirits, it was she who decided who would be slain in battle and then escorted them to her domain in the afterworld.

A late development in northern mythology was the quasi-Goddess Hel who presided over the underworld to which went those who died of old age and disease rather than in battle. Her Saxon counterpart, Holda, was apparently not regarded fearfully but was thought of as a mother calling her tired children home to rest.

As Christianity supplanted pagan cults St. Gertrude of Nevilles, who lived between 629 and 659, was the Christian saint who took over from Hel and Holda the task of gathering up the souls of the dead. She became associated with funerals, and in medieval art she is sometimes shown with a cat in her arms and surrounded by mice which run up her staff. In other illustrations she is actually depicted as a cat. As mice were a medieval symbol for the souls of the dead, people who believed in shape-shifting (the ability magically to change oneself into the form of an animal) would have imagined Gertrude as a cat catching the souls of men. The early bishops prayed to her for help in exterminating the plagues of real mice which periodically ravaged the countryside. In Germany there is still a superstition that the souls of the dead assume the forms of mice, and when the head of a household dies it is said that even the mice of the house abandon it.

If the cat was remembered for Hel, or Hecate who was the Greek Goddess of the Underworld, or for Sekhnet, Bast's lion-headed counterpart who brought sickness and death, it would be natural for people to mistrust it as being a portent of illness and approaching death. A woman from Western Ireland held strong views on the unhealthiness of cats although she did not know their basis. When talking with Lady Gregory she said:

As to cats, they're a class in themselves. They're good to catch mice and rats, but just let them come in and out of the house for that; they're about their own business all the time. And in the old times they could talk. And it's said that the cats gave a shilling for what they have; fourpence that the housekeeper might be careless and leave the milk about that they'd get at it; and fourpence that they'd tread so light that no one would hear them, and fourpence that they'd be able to see in the dark. And I might as well throw out that drop of tea I left on the dresser to cool, for the cat is after that. There might be a hair in it, and the hair of a cat is poison.

To dream of a cat is generally regarded as a bad omen. A book of dream interpretation written in Roman times stated that to dream of being badly scratched by a cat meant sickness and trouble. In Germany it is believed that to dream of a black cat at Christmastime foretells an alarming illness during the coming year.

The sixteenth-century Italian naturalist, Ulisse Aldrovandi, recorded that a howling cat appeared unexpectedly before a dying man and then disappeared, and that a woman whose breast was scratched by a cat took this as an omen of death and died within a few days. If a black cat lies on the bed of a sick man he will surely die. On the other hand, there is a belief that a cat will not remain in the house where someone is about to die. Therefore if the family cat refuses to stay indoors this is regarded as a very bad sign.

If a cat is seen on a grave the buried person's soul must be in the Devil's power. Two cats seen fighting near a dying person, or on the grave shortly after a funeral, are really the Devil and an angel fighting for possession of the soul. Here we see that under Christian pressure the old belief was adapted so that now it was the Devil who wanted the souls of the dead rather than Hel or even St. Gertrude. He could pass before the bed of a dying person in the form of any animal except the lamb which was sacred to Jesus. Most commonly he appeared as a he-goat, a cock or a hen, or a cat. A French proverb from La Creuse says:

The dog wakes three times to watch over his master; the cat wakes three times to strangle him.

Superstitious people of the twentieth century have reported seeing a strange cat, which does not belong to the household and cannot be found afterwards, at the time of the death of a friend or relative. The death does not necessarily have to take place in that house and may happen at a distance, but the time of death always corresponds to the time when the cat appeared.

The Irish say:

Don't never cross a road what a black cat cross't, ain't nothing but sorrow, 'tain't nothing but loss.

A black cat crossing one's path by moonlight means death in an epidemic and in Normandy a tortoise-shell cat climbing a tree foretells death by accident. The latter belief may be connected with this ominous-sounding line:

I have been a spotted-headed cat on a forked tree.

It occurs in a very ancient poem by the Irish bard named Gwion and according to Robert Graves refers to the more sinister life-taking side of a Corn-Goddess who may have been the Celtic counterpart of Demeter identified by the Greeks with the Egyptian Isis and Bast's destructive counterpart, Sekhnet.

This brings us back to the ancient Earth-Mother Frigg, and the 'Corn Spirit' described in Chapter 2, to which the cat was sacrificed at harvest-time. All the earth-mother goddesses, whether Egyptian, Graeco-Roman, Norse, Celtic or Saxon were originally three-in-one figures. They both gave and took life. They supervised the seasonal agricultural round as well as men's lives. All life returned to them at the end. Gradually this primal unity became less important, the Earth-Mother receded and the other two aspects, the lover and destroyer, developed into a pair of opposites. The cat continued to be their symbol, to presage ill health and death and to be a good luck emblem for love and marriage.

7

With heretics and witches

Yet I tell you mickle more;
The cat lieth in the cradle;
I pray you keep true heart in store;
A penny for a ladle.

The above verse is from an anonymous poem described as a 'Nonsense Carol' of the fifteenth century, but whose origins must be much earlier. The whole poem is full of allusions to paganism and witchcraft but here it is enough to point out that the line 'The cat lieth in the cradle' would have evoked in some hearers images of Lilith, a life-taking or vampire-like cat capable of sucking the breath out of a baby.

When Christianity became the official religion of Europe, the priestesses who had administered the old faiths were forced underground. Isis, Artemis, Hecate, Diana, Venus, Freya and Holda and all ideas concerning a 'Great Earth-Mother' who both gave and took life were discredited, and in so far as the cat was their symbol it, too, was despised.

To the Christian the cat was a symbol of laziness and lust. As persecution of the adherents to the old cults intensified it was hard to pass on traditional rituals and beliefs from one generation to the next, and garbled versions and inaccuracies inevitably crept in. Sometimes the old lore was confused due to lack of trained initiates, but sometimes it was done deliberately in order to protect its followers from discovery. Many old songs and jingles which now seem pure nonsense may have begun in this way. To the outsider they would be innocent enough, but the initiated who understood the hidden meanings no doubt took great pleasure in singing such songs publicly and in the hearing of upholders of the new faith.

This conglomeration of muddled traditions is now labelled 'witchcraft', a subject which still fascinates a great many people, reflecting as it does our mixed guilt, nostalgia and horror. Here our only concern with witches is in so far as they and their practices were associated with cats, although there were in fact many animals beside cats, such as goats, dogs, toads and lizards, which played a part in witchcraft.

Witches practised storm-raising around the coast of Scotland and cults of the pagan goddesses were still flourishing in the fifteenth century. Freya was said to appear every night in a chariot drawn by no less than twenty cats, a big increase over the original two which drew her modest cart in the Norse myth. Holda led a procession of virgins either riding astride on tom-cats or disguised in their furs. Till quite recently in Hungary it was commonly believed that cats between the ages of seven and twelve years became witches, and that witches rode on tom-cats, especially black ones. To deliver a cat from the power of a witch it was necessary to make a cross-shaped cut in the cat's skin. In Italy and Germany all cats seen wandering on roof-tops during the month of February were thought to be witches and were shot.

In the tale of 'Tibbs Cat and the Apple-Tree Man' collected by Ruth Tongue in 1910 from an oral tradition of unknown antiquity, the kitten is half curious and half afraid of becoming involved with the witches:

There was a little cat down Tibb's Farm, no much more'n a kitten—a little dairy-maid with a face so clean as a daisy. A pretty little dear she was, but her wanted to know too much. There was fields down along as wasn't liked. No one cared much about working there. Y'see, 'twas all elder there, and there was a queer wind used to blow there most times, and sound like someone talking it would. I wouldn't go there myself unless I had a criss-cross of salt on a crust. Oh! yes, my maid, I could show 'ee the field now, but I don't, and don't you be like Tibb's cat, and go look-see for yourself! There's summat bad about down there, and that was why all they wild black cats goed there on certain nights, and Tibb's cat she wished to go too. She tried to find the way Candlemas Eve, and Allern (Hallowe'en) and all the wisht nights witches do meet, but her weren't big enough to catch up. So, when New Year's Eve came, she tried again.

This time she got as far as the orchet, and then the Apple-Tree Man he called out to her, 'Yew go on back whoame, my dear. There's folk a-coming to pour cider for my roots, and shoot off guns to drive away the witches. This be no place for yew. Yew go back whoame, and don't come awandering round at night till St Tibb's Eve.'

The little dairy-maid her took off home with her tail stiff with vright. Properly scared she, the Apple-Tree Man did. And she never wandered at night again, 'cause she didn't know when St Tibb's Eve is. Nor do anybody else.

The wood of the elder tree was often used to make witches' wands, and 'dairy-maid' was the local word for a white and tortoise-shell cat. The term 'tib-cat' refers to a female. Once in general use it now only survives in the pet names 'Tibbles' and 'Tibby'.

Shakespeare, who linked cats with witches, makes the three witches in *Macbeth* commence their chant as they prepare their evil spell with the words:

Thrice the brindled cat hath mewed.

When an old woman who kept a cat was accused of being a witch the cat was also accused of being her 'familiar'. This meant that the cat, as either the Devil in disguise or as the Devil's emissary, had come to her and by scratching her to draw blood had bound her in a compact with Satan. Witches were also believed to have additional teats from which their familiar could suck. Since kittens taken too young from their mothers often develop the habit of sucking anything resembling a teat, such as a button or a loop of cloth, it is easy to see how this belief gained credence.

Medieval broadsheets, which were comparable to our modern comics, showed horrifying pictures of domestic cats as witches' 'familiars', and children's books until recently were full of illustrations showing witches with their cats. This rhyme of the 1880s about 'Old Judy the Witch of Burwell' represents a widespread attitude:

> *A wicked old crone*
> *Who lived all alone*
> *In a hut beside the reeds*
> *With a high crowned hat*
> *And a black tom-cat,*
> *Whose looks were as black as her deeds.*

John Gay, writing at the beginning of the eighteenth century, could still make the assumption that his readers would know that an old woman who kept cats was in danger of being considered a witch. In his fable called 'The Old Woman and Her Cats' there are these lines:

> *Teaz'd with their cries her choler grew*
> *And thus she sputter'd 'Hence ye crew.*
> *Fool that I was to entertain*
> *Such imps, such fiends, a hellish train!*
> *Had ye been never hous'd and nurst*
> *I, for a witch had n'er been curst.*
> *To you I own, that crouds of boys*
> *Worry me with eternal noise;*
> *Straws laid across my pace retard,*
> *The horse-shoe's nail'd (each threshold's guard)*
> *The stunted broom the wenches hide,*
> *For fear that I should up and ride;*
> *They stick with pins my bleeding seat,*
> *And bid me show my secret teat'.*

The cats reply that they suffer equally from the compact, saying:

> *'Tis infamy to serve a hag;*
> *Cats are thought imps, her broom a nag;*
> *And boys against our lives combine,*
> *Because, 'tis said, your cats have nine.*

As cats are popular pets for old women they naturally figure frequently in descriptions of witches' familiars. But it must be emphasized that any animal kept by an old woman could qualify.

Witches were not always women and a male witch or 'warlock' might also have a special relationship with the cat. The ceremonies carried out at the Witches' Sabbat in time became labelled as Devil-worship. At these meetings the male warlock or his cat impersonated the Devil who was worshipped by the female witches. Thus the cat played more than one role at a Sabbat. In one account the witches arrived disguised as black cats and later, while the Devil presided, women with cats tied to their petticoats danced and shouted.

Descriptions of witches' Sabbats in which the participants kiss the Devil's arse while he is in the form of a black cat are common. Sometimes the Devil was impersonated by a man dressed in cat-skins and perhaps wearing a cat-mask, and at other times a real cat was used. A fifteenth-century writer, La Franc, tells of an old woman who from the age of sixteen went regularly to assemblies where a crowd of women gazed upon the Devil who would be in the form of a cat or a he-goat. She said 'They kissed his arse as a sign of obedience'.

Unfortunately no one was interested in writing down exactly what went on at Sabbats until the times of the great witch-hunts and then the accounts were either obtained by torture or were so prejudiced as to be practically useless. The first known written record of the Devil disguised as a cat is from a witch trial in Guernsey in 1563. As late as 1767 in Lapland the Devil was said to appear at the Sabbat as a cat, handling the celebrants from their feet to their mouths and counting their teeth. A modern account of proceedings at a Sabbat is provided by a Spanish doctor who came accidentally across such an occasion as recently as 1942 in the Basque country near the French border:

At eleven o'clock at night on an unspecified day of the week various people were together on a farm, eating and drinking copiously. . . . The party was held in a barn which had a wooden upper floor and loft. It consisted of the lady of the house and six men and two more women. In spite of the heat, logs were

burning in the central space . . . at the command of the master
of ceremonies . . . they all undressed completely. . . . After a
period of increasing merriment, the mistress of the house took
a cauldron of soup into the barn and placed it on the embers.
Then the leader, climbing up into the loft of the barn, threw
down a live cat into the cauldron, which was immediately
covered with a lid by someone else.

The cat soup was communally eaten with much ritual.
Between spoonfuls some sort of spell, litany or incantation was
recited in the Basque tongue.

A seventeenth-century treatise on German witches connected
their activities with the Valkyries who Freya led because the
principal celebrations of both took place on May Eve. After
anointing themselves with the fat of cats or wolves, ass's milk
and other unspecified ingredients, the witches were able to fly off
on broomsticks to feast with the Devil. On the night of May Eve
all German witches were transported to Blocksberg, the old name
of the highest peak in the Harz Mountains, where they spent the
night in feasting and dancing with their lovers.

When cats gathered together they were often thought to be
witches themselves. From the French district of Indre it is
reported that a Sabbat of black cats took place at the foot of a
cross, but that cats with the slightest trace of rust or brown in
their coats were excluded as not being truly representative of the
Devil. In the old French province of Maine cats had to be at least
eight years old to attend the annual Sabbat. This agrees with the
Hungarian belief that cats from the age of seven to twelve were
witches.

At Finistère, Advent was the time when cats left the house at
nightfall and gathered at squares and cross-roads to howl at each
other. Peasants returning home late at night reported hearing
these cats swearing and blaspheming 'in the Christian tongue',
which was presumably French. That these occurrences took place
at cross-roads, squares and where crosses were set up reminds us
of Hecate, Goddess of the Underworld, whose image, guarded
by cats, was placed at cross-roads where her worshippers left

offerings on the eve of the full moon. Another old French record tells of a man who buried a black cat in a box at a cross-roads with enough bread soaked in holy water and holy oil to keep it alive for three days. He had then intended to dig it up, kill it and make a belt from its skin which he expected would confer on him the power of second sight. Unfortunately for him the cat was discovered by dogs and he was tried for witchcraft.

Although these practices may at first have been addressed to a goddess they were soon appropriated by the Devil. A book called *L'Evangile du Diable* or *The Devil's Bible* says that the Devil invited all the cats to feast with him on Shrove Tuesday, which was why it was so rare to see a cat on that day. For the rest of the year the Devil apparently kept them fully employed:

> Only imbeciles do not know that all cats have a pact with the Devil. . . . You can understand why cats sleep or pretend to sleep all day long, beside the fire in winter or in the sun in the summer. It is their task to patrol the barns and stables all night, to see everything, to hear everything. And you can deduce from that why the Evil Spirits, warned just in time, always manage to vanish away, to disappear before we can see them.

The book also contains a recipe for making oneself invisible:

> Take a black cat, a new cooking pot and an agate stone. Draw water from a fountain at midnight. Place the cat in the pot, hold the lid down firmly with the left hand and boil for 24 hours. Place the meat in a new dish, throw it over your left shoulder and watch yourself till you no longer see yourself in a mirror.

In 1232 Pope Gregory IX sent a Papal Bull to the bishops in the region of Oldenburg, Lower Saxony, because the people of Stedingerland in the area had been refusing to pay their tithes and had assaulted the clergy who came to collect them. The Church accused these people of forming a secret society in which they were in league with the Devil to persecute the faithful, despise the sacraments, make waxen images and consult witches. The Papal Bull described how on certain nights the people assembled . . .

> Then all sit down to a banquet and when they rise after it is

finished, a black cat emerges from a kind of statue which normally stands in the place where these meetings are held. It is large as a fair-sized dog, and enters backwards with its tail erect. First the novice kisses its hind parts, then the Master of Ceremonies proceeds to do the same and finally all the others in turn; or rather all those who deserve the honour. The rest, that is those who are not worthy of this favour, kiss the Master of Ceremonies. When they have returned to their places they stand in silence for a few minutes with heads turned towards the cat. Then the Master says: 'Forgive us.' The person standing behind him repeats this and a third adds, 'Lord we know it.' A fourth person ends the formula by saying, 'We shall obey.'

This was followed by a sexual orgy and afterwards . . .

When these horrors have taken place the lamps are lit again and everyone regains their places. Then, from a dark corner, the figure of a man emerges. The upper part of his body from the hips upwards shines as brightly as the sun but below that his skin is coarse and covered with fur like a cat.

These people may have belonged to a cult in which the cat was acting as a symbol of the sun and the moon. That the top half of the man's body shone 'as brightly as the sun' while the lower part was 'covered with fur like a cat' symbolized the brightness of day contrasted with the dark enveloping night. The form which the worship took is reminiscent of the Tantric sects of Buddhism and Hinduism which involved ritual sex and the lifting of all taboos and restraints. But since all the old goddesses were in one of their aspects concerned with love and fertility, perhaps it is not necessary to look further afield to explain these ceremonies.

Besides the people who continued to practice the ancient cults now labelled witchcraft, there were heretical groups such as Albigenses, Cathars, and Waldensians who were widespread in Europe, especially the South of France. They were sects of the Manichees, a dualist religion which opposed Christianity and asserted that good and evil balanced each other in the world. Their Christian persecutors said Satan presided over their midnight ceremonies in the form of a large black cat. They were accused of holding meetings like those of a witches' Sabbat. Hymns were sung till first night-watch when, it was said, a black cat was lowered into their midst as a signal for the lights to be put out. General licence then ensued. During the thirteenth century these groups were systematically exterminated and their property confiscated. The charge against the Cathars made in a Papal Bull by Pope Gregory was that they 'kissed Lucifer in the form of a black cat' and that they bred black cats, that is, cats the colour of 'evil and shame'. It must have been of similar practices that the Knights Templar were accused when in 1307 Philip IV of France accused them of various satanic practices including worshipping cats. Whether the charges were justified or not it is very interesting that in the Maison des Templiers at Metz there is a wood carving of a cat and a sow holding a hymn book while an ass, a fox and a unicorn play musical instruments.

That the cat continued to be assocated with evil in the Christian mind is emphasized by the sixteenth-century religious paintings of Tintoretto and the Florentine, Ghirlandajo. Both put a cat into their painting of *The Last Supper*. In Ghirlandajo's it sits broodingly by Judas. In Tintoretto's *Annunciation*, a fiendish-looking cat watches the proceedings from under a cloud. In some places suspicion continued into the twentieth century. When H. G. Wells lived in the South of France he used to take his black cat with him on walks. If frightened, it would jump up on his shoulder till the danger was passed. The French peasants who saw them thought the cat was unholy and although they never harmed it they would go out of their way to avoid passing them closely.

There seems to have been some confusion in the public mind as to whether witches merely disguised themselves in cat-skins, or whether they actually turned into cats. Among the Basques, witches were thought to take on the form of birds, cats, foxes or asses in order to place a spell in the right place and leave the scene again undetected. At a witch trial in 1586 a woman from Bergheim, near Cologne, was accused of disguising herself in the skins of a black cat in order to enter another person's room to do him harm. Until recently in parts of Germany it was believed that old women had the power to turn themselves into black cats so as to slip more easily into barns to put spells upon cattle.

A magic spell recited to turn oneself into a cat was:

I shall goe intill ane catt
With sorrow, and sych, and a blak shot.

And to return to human form one recited:

Cat, cat God send thee a blak shott
I am a cat's likeness just now,
But I sal be in a womanis likeness ewin now.

There is an echo of this chant in the English folk song called 'The Coal Black Smith' or 'The Two Magicians' where the Maiden and the Smith go through a series of animal transformations until finally the Smith captures the Maiden. An older version of this song stems from a time when an earth-mother goddess was worshipped. Then it was the Maid, as a personification or a priestess of the goddess, who overcame any danger that might threaten the crops; the danger itself was personified by the male Devil or the Smith. The song would have accompanied a mime or dance at a Sabbat. Robert Graves gives us this restoration of the last verse:

Yet I shall go into a mouse
And haste me unto the miller's house,
There in his corn to have good game
Ere that I be fetched hame.
    —Mouse, take heed of a white tib-cat
That never was baulked of mouse or rat,
For I'll crack thy bones in Our Lady's name:
Thus shall thou be fetched hame.

'To fetch home again' meant to return to one's normal shape. Of course the poem can be read on two levels, the superficial one warning a mouse of a cat that is a good mouser, and the underlying meaning referring to the old Mother Goddess who as guardian of the earth's fruitfulness, would have been invoked to protect the harvest from mice. In this sense the Devil is thought of as being a shape-shifter who transforms himself into a mouse in order to steal the grain while the Goddess in cat-form protects it. It is interesting to compare these shape-shifting abilities of the Maid and the Smith, or the Goddess and the Devil with the story in *The Arabian Nights* of the Jinnee and the Princess reported on p. 53. The Arabian tale is presented as a mixture of magic and court intrigue but in its original form it must have been based on similar traditions of ritual associated with the safety of the harvest.

Many surnames in rural France are said to reflect the ability once claimed by some people to turn themselves into cats to exert evil power and the Irish also believed that human beings could roam at night in the form of cats. Lady Gregory was told:

> There's something not right about cats. Steve Smith says he knew a keeper that shot one, and it went into a sort of a heap, and when he came near, it spoke, and he found it was some person, and it said it had to walk its seven acres. And there's some have heard them together at night talking Irish.

But by the twentieth century this belief only persisted in remote rural areas. An old man writing in 1963 of his boyhood in the Cambridgeshire fens said:

> Everyone in those days that lived around my home held firm belief in the power witches possessed, and a lot of good food us children would have been glad to have was wasted by being placed outside the door for a wandering witch to collect for her supper, who never appeared in human form. Any seen were disguised as cats or rats, and it was a well-known fact the dish the food was placed in needed no washing up next morning, it was so clean. My father, who was in great demand as a lay preacher in the Fen chapels, firmly believed that stewed pigs' brains served on a plate which had contained the witches' supper (unwashed) gave him such power to preach in his sermons that it caused his listeners to sit enthralled.

If women can turn themselves into cats in order to go abroad at night on unlawful pursuits, it seems logical to assume that if some injury happens to them while they are in cat-form then that injury will persist after they return to their human shape. There are many blood-curdling stories based on this theme. A Spanish tale tells of a man who noticed that when he put fresh milk out on the window-sill to keep it cool at night some of it always disappeared in a suspicious way. One night he decided to keep watch and hid by the window. Soon a black cat appeared, jumped on the sill and began quietly to lap the milk. In a rage he threw open the window and hit the cat with a stick on the front leg as it tried to get away. The cat seemed to cry out with a human voice as it was struck, and then disappeared. Next morning it was discovered that an old woman in the next village had one arm bandaged. She claimed to have fallen downstairs, but the man knew well enough that she was the cat who had stolen his milk.

In Arkansas the Ozarks tell a story of a drunkard who accepted a bet to spend the night in a house which had once been used by witches. At midnight when the whisky jar was empty and as he was just falling asleep an enormous cat appeared, howling and spitting at him. Taking aim with his pistol he shot it. There was a woman's scream and as the candle went out he saw a foot with blood dripping from it going over the window-ledge. Next day he was told that a woman who lived near-by had accidentally shot her foot off and died from loss of blood.

Another Ozark story, collected by Isabel Carter, tells how Jack hired himself out as a miller to a mill where nobody had ever survived a night . . .

'Bedads, I'll get along all right,' says Jack. So Jack baked some bread un made him some coffee un fried him some meat. All at once, the little cabin got dark as midnight. Jack got up and stirred his fire, and when he looked round, every crack in the house was full of cats—jest as thick as they could stick—with their eyes jest shining.

That sort of scared Jack, and he jest set down and commenced to eaten'. All of a sudden one big old black cat hollered, 'Sop, doll, sop'. Then all the cats sat down on the floor. She walked up and popped her paw in his meat sop and licket hit and hollered, 'Sop doll, sop'. Jack said, 'Stick your old paw in here again and I'll whack it off.'

She did hit again and he hacked it off. When he hacked it off, it fell into the fryin' pan—hit was a woman's hand, with a ring on the finger, and she hollered 'Whar-a-a,' and all them cats went out through the cracks and the moon shined back in as bright as day. So he tuk that hand and he wrops hit up in some tissue paper and drops hit down in his coat pocket.

Next morning he wuz up bright and early and had his breakfast over and was grinding and whistling when the miller cames down. Said, 'Why, hello, Jack, I see you're still alive.'

'Yes, bedads, I'm still alive,' says Jack. And he told all about the cats, and pulled this hand out of his pocket and handed it to the man.

He says, 'Hit's my wife's hand.'

Jack says, 'O surely not.'

He says, 'Yes, hit is.'

Jack says, 'Well, she was a big black cat when I hacked it off.'

'Well, hit is,' says the Miller, 'fer this is a ring I put on her hand yesterday.' So he tuk the hand and went up to the house. Says, 'Nancy, let's see your right hand.'

She poked out her left. Says, 'Nancy, hit's yer right hand I want.'

She begin cryin' and said, 'I haven't any.'

So he says, 'Now tell me all about this, Nancy, and I won't have you burned.'

'Well I didn't want you to have a miller. I wanted you keep the mill yourself. So I got all my friends, and witched 'em into cats, and we put pizen into the millers' sop. And when I went to put pizen into this man's sop, he hacked off my hand.'

So the miller gathered up all the other witches and had 'em burned, and that made the other husbands mad, and they had his wife hung. He wouldn't let 'em burn her, 'cause he had said she shouldn't be. So Jack made an end of a good many witches.

Other shape-shifting stories involve women suspected of being unfaithful to their husbands who leave home at night in the form of a cat. An example of this is the French tale, *La Chatte de la Croix des Haies*. One evening a young man was returning from courting the woman who was to be his wife. He saw at the foot of the cross called *La Croix des Haies* a beautiful white cat who miaowed tenderly and rubbed against his legs. From then on until he married, the cat always met him at this spot. Months passed and he forgot his encounters with the cat. Then one night he awoke with a start to find himself alone in the bed. At dawn his wife returned and slipped quietly in beside him again. Getting no answers to his questioning he sulked but went to bed as usual. Again she disappeared. How could she get out when the door was bolted? Finally one night he saw a small white paw slip through the crack of the door to reach the bolt. He took a mighty blow at it with his hatchet. There was a terrible scream and his wife did not reappear for eight days. When she did return he found her hand had been chopped off at the wrist.

Cats did not always get the worst of these encounters. In 1566 at a place called Kernon in France, a group of sorcerers used to meet in an old abandoned château. The villagers were uneasy about this and decided to drive them out. They went to the château at midnight but there they were met by a horde of cats which attacked them, killing some and wounding others. Obviously the cats were the sorcerers who had assumed cat-shape.

These surviving scraps of information about cults and superstitions in which cats played a part offer us a glimpse of what were once widespread organized religious systems in Europe. Witchcraft, a conglomeration of confused traditions, marked the pathetic end to a varied assortment of practices. Besides the heretical sects who were smeared with the taint of witchcraft by their enemies, there were followers of cults who worshipped goddesses such as Freya, Diana and Hecate as well as many local divinities whose names have been forgotten.

Whether the downfall of goddess worship was due entirely to the spread and dominance of Christianity we do not know. It may have already been on the decline because a patriarchal social organization had replaced the ancient matriarchal one, but in either case it is not of central importance. Our concern is to attempt to distinguish the role played by the cat or the cat-image during the many transformations which have affected and altered beliefs and ideas since a distinct European tradition differentiated itself. Whatever the underlying reasons were we shall see that the cat became associated with a mythical male figure at first described as a 'Cat-King' who later, under the impact of Christianity, became the Devil.

8

Becoming a king

Cats are a mysterious kind of folk.
There is more passing in their minds
than we are aware of.
(SIR WALTER SCOTT)

In the last chapter we saw that the supposed abilities of witches to turn themselves into cats was based upon a belief in an earth mother goddess who could appear in the form of a cat in order to guard the harvest. The older version of the song called 'The Coal Black Smith' preserves the memory of a matriarchal society in which a mime was enacted of a goddess in the form of a cat killing an evil magician who menaced the crops in the form of a mouse. Later the song was adapted and changed to suit the needs of a patriarchal society and the Smith or Magician became the winner.

This change is typical of many which overtook the cat who had been sacred to a goddess. We are fortunate that so much folk-lore which throws light upon the process of these changes has survived in the remoter parts of Europe such as Ireland, Scotland and the Isle of Man. In these places we can still find the vestiges of beliefs which have disappeared elsewhere. They show that stories and traditions about the cat became attached to a male figure and that the goddesses dwindled in size and importance, a fact which was expressed by their transformation in belief and story into fairies.

A tale from the West of Ireland of how a black hound dog killed a cat shows traces of very old roots. Is it describing in mythic terms the overthrow of the cat as a symbol of a goddess by the male element represented by the black hound dog?

90

There was a man had a house full of children, and one day he was taking their measure for boots. And the cat that was sitting on the hearth said, 'Take my measure for a pair of boots along with the rest.' So the man did, and when he went to the shoe-maker he told him of what the cat said. And there was a man in the shop at the time, and he having two grey-hounds with him, and one of them all black without a single white hair. And he said, 'Bring the cat here tomorrow. You can tell it that the boots can't be made without it coming for its measure.' So the next day he brought the cat in a bag, and when he got to his shop the man was there with his greyhounds, and he let the cat out, and it praying him not to loosen the bag. And it made away through the fields and the hounds after it, and whether it killed one of them I don't know, but anyhow the black hound killed it, the one that had not a white hair on its body.

That the black hound had not a single white hair on its body is a sure sign that there was something supernatural about it.

A faint and confused recollection of the period when a male symbol was replacing the old matriarchal ones is supplied by W. B. Yeats who records that the Irish believed that demons could transform themselves into black dogs and white cats. The passage of time and the pressure of Christianity have resulted in this male symbol being described as a demon. The roof painting in St. Mary's church at Bury St. Edmunds of a black dog springing at a white cat could also illustrate the same tale.

Although in these examples the male element is represented by a dog which attacks the matriarchal goddess who is still symbolized by a cat, it is not long before the cat transfers itself to the new male-orientated system of ideas and appears as 'The King of the Cats'.

Tales of a 'King of the Cats' have been recorded from many parts of the British Isles and Europe. These cats may appear to be sleeping by the fireside but they are in fact listening to all that is said and are ever ready to resume their kingly duties. Washington Irvine recalled that as he and Sir Walter Scott contemplated a sombre tabby which sat attentively with them by the fire, Scott began to tell a tale about . . .

. . . a gude man who was returning to his cottage one night, when, in a lonely out-of-the-way place, he met with a funeral procession of cats all in mourning, bearing one of their race to the grave in a coffin covered with a black velvet pall. The worthy man, astonished and half frightened at so strange a pageant, hastened home and told what he had seen to his wife and children. Scarce had he finished, when a great black cat that sat beside the fire raised himself up, exclaimed, 'Then I am the King of the Cats!' and vanished up the chimney. The funeral seen by the gude man was one of the cat dynasty.

More detailed is this traditional version quoted by Katherine Briggs:

They say that two young men were once staying in a remote hunting lodge in the Highlands, and one of them had been overtired the day before and chose to stay at home while the other went out shooting. He returned late at night, and all through supper was very quiet and absent, but afterwards, when they were sitting by the fire with the old, black household cat between them, the young man said: 'A strange thing happened to me this evening, I lost my way home, that's why I'm so late, and it fell dark whilst I was still wandering about. At last I saw a light in the distance, and made towards it, thinking it might be some cottage where I could ask my way; but when I got to it I saw that it came streaming out of a hollow oak. Look at that cat!' he said, breaking off. 'I'll swear he understands every word I'm saying.' And indeed, the old cat was looking steadily at him with a very knowing air.

'Never mind the cat,' said his friend. 'What happened?'

'I climbed up the tree and looked down inside. It was much bigger than it looked, and furnished like a kind of church. I was looking down and heard a kind of wailing sound, like singing and howling, and a procession came up into the place —a funeral, a coffin and mourners all in black with torches, but the queer thing was that the mourners were all cats, and they were all wailing and howling together; and on the coffin there was a crown and sceptre—,' But he got no further, for the old cat had started up, and suddenly shouted—'By Jove, old Peter's dead and I'm King of the Cats!' At that he was up the chimney in a flash, and was never seen again.

An Irish variant harks back to a time when the cat in the story was female, for whoever 'Lady Betty' might have been, her place had not yet been usurped by a 'King':

There was an uncle of mine near Galway, and one night his wife was very sick, and he had to go to the village to get something for her. And it's a very lonely road, and as he was going what should he see but a great number of cats, walking along the road, and they were carrying a young cat, and crying over it.

And when he was on his way home again from the village he met them again, and one of the cats turned and spoke to him like a person would, and said, 'Bid Lady Betty to come to the funeral or she'll be late.' So he ran home in a great fright, and he couldn't speak for some time after getting back to the house, but sat there by the fire in a chair. And at last he began to tell his wife what had happened. And when he said that he had met a cat's funeral, his own cat that was sleeping by the hearth began to stir her tail, and looked up at him affectionate like. But when he got to where he was bid send Lady Betty to the funeral, she made one dash at his face and scraped it, she was so mad that she wasn't told at once. And then she began to tear at the door, that they had to let her out.

A Lancashire version has lost much of its supernatural impact and the dead cat is named 'Mally Dixon' which is surely a comic corruption of 'Malediction'.

The Irish firmly believed that on a certain night of the year all the cats in the neighbourhood gathered to fight and afterwards returned home considerably the worse for wear. Perhaps they and the Kilkenny Cats who according to legend fought until only their tails remained were fighting for the kingly succession:

Becoming a king

There wanst was two cats in Kilkenny,
Aitch thought there was once cat too many;
So they quarrelled and fit,
They scratched and they bit,
Till, excepting their nails
And the tips of their tails,
Instead of two cats, there wasn't any.

The *Ancient Legends of Ireland* collected by F. S. Wilde, preserve the tale of Seanchan, Chief Poet of Ireland, who satirized the King of the Cats and nearly lost his life. Although the story that has come down to us has been modernized so that the Irish chieftains drink French wine and the bard is saved by a Saint, yet when the King of the Cats arrives at court to fetch Seanchan it is clear that this is no ordinary cat:

> Now when it was told to Seanchan that the King of the Cats was on his way to come and kill him, he was timorous, and besought Guaire and all the nobles to stand by and protect him. And before long a vibrating, impressive, impetuous sound was heard, like a raging tempest of fire in full blaze. And when the cat appeared he seemed to them of the size of a bullock; and this was his appearance—rapacious, panting, jagged-eared, snub-nosed, sharp-toothed, nimble, angry vindictive, glare-eyed, terrible, sharp-clawed. Such was his similitude. But he passed on amongst them, not minding till he came to Seanchan; and him he seized by the arm and jerked him up on his back, and made off the way he came before any one could touch him; for he had no other object in view but to get hold of the poet.

According to Robert Graves this Cat-King lived at the Knowth burial mound in County Meath. The tale goes back to a time when kings still had mythical qualities and when history and legend were not clearly distinguished. A similar figure was a slender black cat who reclined on a silver chair in a cave at Clough in Connaught. Before St. Patrick's arrival in Ireland it made oracular pronouncements and abused anyone who tried to deceive it.

As late as the tenth century A.D. King Caibre of Ireland was described as 'Cat-Headed' which suggests that his ancestors worshipped God in the form of a cat, and that as Priest-Kings they would have worn a cat-mask at ceremonies. Charmingly naïve but perhaps containing a trace of faintly-remembered ritual from a time when the king impersonated the deity, is the view expressed by an 'old Scottish writer' of unknown date, that the anointing of a king at his coronation would have bound him to his kingdom in the same way that buttering a cat's paws keeps it from wandering away from a new home:

> But do ye ken the freet of you doing wi' the oil on the palms of the hand? It's may opinion that it's an ancient charm to keep the new king in the kingdom: for there's no surer way to make a cat stay at hame than to creesh her paws in like manner.

In old Pictish Scotland, from Bronze Age times down to about A.D. 700, chieftains had animal badges which may have originally been the totem animal of their tribe. For instance, the Earl of Sutherland was once the paramount chief of the Old Clan Chattan, the 'Cat People', who had a mountain cat as their crest. The Earl was then known as 'Mohr ar chat' or 'The Great Cat'. The Scots county of Caithness is said to derive its name from Teutonic settlers of the tribe called Catti so that it was at first known as 'Catti-ness', and a tribe in the Low Countries was called 'The Friends of the Cat' but quite what was meant by this title is hard to tell.

Of interest here is the legend which explains how cats first reached Scotland. When the Egyptian army was defeated General Galsthelos fled with his beautiful wife Scota, a daughter of Pharoah, to the far end of the Mediterranean. They established a kingdom called Brigantium in what is now Compostella, Portugal. Scota took her cats with her and centuries later Fergus I, a descendant of Galsthelos and Scota, took cats with him when he became ruler of a kingdom further north. This kingdom he named Scotland in memory of his ancestress. If there is any truth at all in this tale it would have been to Ireland that the cats went with Fergus. It was not till much later, in the fifth century, that the Irish, who were then known as Scotti, began to penetrate into what was then Pictish territory, and made it Scotland.

On the Isle of Man there are stories of a 'Cat-King' who lives the life of an ordinary house cat during the day but at night assumes his regal status and travels the lanes in fiery splendour. It behoves the householder to look after this cat well or it may take its revenge. But the Isle of Man cats are also in league with the fairies who accept them because they are able to see ghosts and wraiths after dark. This is why, it is said, the cat is the only member of the Manx family allowed to stay when the fairies come into the kitchen at night. In fact, if the family has put the cat out before going to bed the fairies will let it in again during the night. In a Scandinavian version of the 'King of the Cats' tale the cat is described as a fairy who has taken on animal form temporarily. Here is evidence of the cat being a 'king' in communities which also preserved tales of its connections with fairies.

We have seen that the goddesses dwindled in importance. This fact was expressed mythically by reducing them in size and portraying them as fairies. Folk beliefs from Ireland and the Isle of Man which imply that cats *are* fairy folk is the culmination of this process. Katherine Briggs in her book *The Fairies in Tradition and Literature* says 'there are many creatures which seem to be animals but which are really fairies in animal form; . . . weasels, cats and toads are often not what they appear. . . .' A view supported by this West of Ireland informant who said:

> For cats is faeries, and every night they're obliged to travel over seven acres; that's why you hear them crying about the country. It was an old woman at the strand told me that, and she should know, for she lived to be a hundred years of age.

Another tale preserved in *Ancient Legends of Ireland* is also about a fairy cat. An old woman was sitting up late to spin when there came several knocks at her cottage door. She asked once or twice who it was and at length a little voice replied:

'Ach, Judy agrah, let us in, for I'm cold and hungry.' She opened the door, and a black cat walked in, followed by two white kittens. The old woman said not a word, good or bad, but sat down to her spinning while the cats washed themselves by the fire and purred loudly. At length the black cat spoke, and warned old Judy to leave off her spinning and be off to bed, for she had already hindered the fairies of their night's pleasure.

'And if it hadn't been for myself and my daughters,' she said, 'it's dead you'd be now. But you've behaved very civil to us, so give us a drink of milk and we'll be off, and mind you don't sit up late again.'

At that old Judy fetched a good bowl of milk; the cats lapped it up, and then shot off up the chimney. But something shone bright in the ashes, and when Judy picked it up it was a silver coin big enough to pay her for many a night's spinning. After that she followed the black cat's advice and never sat up late again.

There is an old Irish saying that:

There's crocks of gold in all the forths, but there's cats and things guarding them.

These forths are the prehistoric burial mounds which are found all over Ireland. They were built by the Danaans, a people whose power traditionally is supposed to have been broken when the ancestors of the modern Irish arrived about 1000 B.C. The Danaans withdrew underground and now inhabit the mounds as 'fairy folk'.

Two of the sites identified as places where cults of Cat-Kings took place in Ireland are a burial mound and a cave. Both in tradition and poetry caves are openings which lead to the underworld and a burial mound is surely to be considered as the antechamber of the underworld. It is also noteworthy that some naturalists think the domestic cat was first taken to Ireland together with new religious beliefs during the Bronze Age. The 'crocks of gold' guarded by cats in Ireland may be part of the same system of belief which assigned cats to guard the treasure buried at cross-roads for Hecate, Goddess of the Underworld. Gradually these places, which housed ritual objects rather than merely golden treasure, became the sanctuary of a Cat-King. Originally the sacred places would have belonged to the Danaans who, it was believed, became reduced in size and with their goddesses were finally transformed into fairies.

Now let us consider this curious tale which comes from the West of Ireland. It purports to be the story of an Irishman who set out to go by ship to America. After the ship had started it had to put into land for repairs. 'In the country where they landed he saw a forth, and he went into it, and there he saw the smallest people he ever saw, and they were the Danes that went out of Ireland; and it was foxes they had for dogs, and weasels were their cats.'

When he returned to the shore he found that the ship had gone without him so he returned to the forth where he met a young man who asked him if he would help his father who was ill in bed. When the old man heard that the stranger was from Ireland he offered him a big reward if he would return there and bring him something out of 'Hacket Hill' which he said would make him as young as his son. The Irishman agreed to help and a ship was prepared. Then the old man gave him these instructions:

'. . . buy a little pig in Galway', he said, 'and bring it to the mouth of the forth of Castle Hacket and roast it there. And inside the forth is an enchanted cat that is keeping guard there, and it will come out; and here is a shotgun and some cross-money that will kill any faery or any enchanted thing. And within in the forth,' he said, 'you will find a bottle and a rack-comb, and bring them back here to me.'

So the man went back to Ireland and carried out the instructions. He roasted the pig in front of the forth and when the cat emerged he shot at it with the cross-money and the cat went away. When he took the bottle and the comb back the old man drank from the bottle and combed his hair with the comb and became as young as his own son.

Becoming a king

Although the reference to America and the fact that the Danaans are mistakenly called Danes makes this tale seem of recent origin, it must be a very old tale in a new setting. As we saw, the Danaans lived on as fairy folk and in the story an enchanted cat guards their forth. The magic comb has associations with combing out, cleaning or purifying so that youth may be restored. It may refer to an actual magical practice or it may represent a nostalgic yearning, still preserved in story, for a return to Danaan times when Ireland was young. That the Danaans' cats were weasels suggests that their word for weasel was later transferred to mean 'cat' as it was in Greek. Robert Graves identifies the Goddess of the Danaans with traditions from Wales, Ireland and Cornwall of a corn-goddess in the form of a sow who was reputed to have given birth to a kitten which grew up to be one of the so-called 'three plagues of Anglesea'. This would explain why a pig had to be roasted outside the forth to bring out the cat.

From hints such as these which have survived in the Celtic fringes of Europe we see how the cat, once sacred to a goddess, was transformed into a 'King of the Cats'. The old stories were adapted and retold with a 'Cat-King' as protagonist but after the arrival of Christianity he did not long enjoy this new status unchallenged: it proved to be but a very short step from Cat-King to the Devil.

9

Between the Devil and the Church

There was a Young Person of Smyrna,
Whose grandmother threatened to burn her;
  But she seized on the cat,
  And said, 'Granny, burn that!
You incongruous old woman of Smyrna!'
(EDWARD LEAR)

When the Devil took human shape in the Isle of Skye he always wore boots and gloves so it was hard to tell whether he had cloven hoofs or claws. But on the shore there are marks on the rocks where he is said to have sharpened his claws. They are exactly like the marks made by a cat on a chair or a table-leg but bigger and deeper.

'Cat-Kings' who had once been consulted as oracles suffered the same fate as their female counterparts who had lingered on with the witches. When they met with the opposition of the Church they were condemned as manifestations of the Devil and the methods by which their aid was sought suffered a corresponding deterioration. In the Scottish Highlands the 'King of the Cats', a huge animal, appeared only to those who were prepared to carry out a diabolical ritual called 'Taigheirm'. This word means either 'armoury' or 'the cry of cats'; it was literally the shrieks of the cats which were the weapons by which the Devil was coerced into granting the celebrant's wishes. Black cats, symbolic of darkness, were collected. The ritual began at midnight between Friday and Saturday and for the duration of the ceremony, over four whole days and nights, the participants, who ate no food, slowly roasted alive a succession of cats on a spit. As soon as one animal died it was replaced by another. Only those with iron nerves could hope to complete successfully the full four-day ritual. For the entire time, in the face of the appalling screams of the burning cats, there must never be a pause in the proceedings. This has given rise to the expression in the Inner Hebrides:

Whatever you see or hear, keep the cat turning.

The continuous torture of their chosen animals caused all the devils to converge on the area. With horrible howls they assembled in the form of black cats till finally one enormous cat appeared. The ritual was now complete and the operators could ask what they wished of the Devil. This might be for wealth or heirs, but most often the gift of second sight was asked for. If granted it would last throughout the lifetime of the successful celebrant.

One of the last occasions when this ritual was performed was in Mull about 1750. Two brothers, Lachlain and Allan Maclean, carried it out. At the end of the fourth day a huge black cat with fire flaming from its eyes was seen sitting on the roof beam of the barn. It let out a frightful howl that could be heard clear across the Strait of Mull to Morvern. Allan who was completely exhausted could only gasp out 'prosperity' but his younger brother Lachlain asked for heirs and wealth. Each was granted his wish. Years later at Allan's funeral, those in the churchyard who had the gift of second sight said they could clearly see Lachlain, who had died earlier, standing in the distance, fully armed, at the head of a host of black cats.

The same magical principle, to blackmail the Devil into granting one's wish by cruelly treating his chosen animal, the one in whose form he can appear, was the basis for a recipe reported by the *Sunday Express* during a witch scare in County York, Pennsylvania in 1929:

To make peace with the devil plunge a live black cat into boiling water, keeping the last bone (of the tail?) as an amulet.

Although it is given as a means of making peace with the Devil, it would have been a peace enforced by threat.

One of the clearest examples of the way in which pagan customs came to be regarded as 'devilish' is Sir James Frazer's description in *The Golden Bough* of a Celtic ritual which evolved into the custom of burning cats at certain times of the year.

In Celtic Europe there were annual ceremonies at which human beings and animals were put in cages made of withies and burned alive on huge bonfires. Their purpose was to ensure the fertility of the fields. The rites usually took place at midsummer or at the beginning of spring but in some places the fires were lit at what is now Hallowe'en. Gradually the human sacrifice was replaced by an animal one and the animal sacrificed was most commonly the cat.

In Christian times the most popular cat-burnings took place on the Eve of St. John which is also Midsummer Eve. Originally the Church had opposed these pagan rites and as early as the seventh century St. Eloi had tried unsuccessfully to stop a celebration in Paris where twenty-four cats were burned alive. But after 1471 these ritual burnings were so thoroughly accepted that it was customary for them to be attended by the French kings. The ceremony in Paris took place at the Place de Grève where the basket of cats was hung from a pole erected in the centre of the bonfire. The spectators afterwards collected the embers from the fire to take home as good luck emblems. During the reign of Henry IV the Dauphine pleaded with his father for the rite to be stopped, but it was still continuing forty years later when, garlanded with roses, Louis XIV attended what was to be the last of these ceremonies and lit the fire himself.

Similar sacrifices were performed at Metz, Lorraine and Luxemburg. Cats were burned alive on Shrove Tuesday in the Vosges, in the Easter bonfires in Alsace and in the Department of Ardennes on the first Sunday in Lent. At Gap in the Department of the High Alps cats were roasted in the midsummer bonfire. Finding it could not stamp out the custom the Church followed its usual policy of connecting pagan customs with the Devil. The ritual burning of cats continued but now it was taught that the cat symbolized the Devil and was being burned, especially if the traditional event took place at Easter or during Lent, to purify the community from his evil influence.

Although the traditional cat-burning at Metz must have gone

back to pagan Celtic times a medieval tale is told to account for it. Once when Metz was in the grip of an epidemic of St. Vitus's dance, a pious knight-at-arms arrived in the town. Being curious he took a room at an inn where he could observe the strange antics of the dancing townsfolk. Later, resting on his bed, he saw in the fire-place a very large and intensely black cat. It stared fixedly at him with gold eyes that flamed and flickered in the firelight. The knight, always eager to battle evil, leapt to his feet, crossed himself and seized his sword. But the sight of the knight crossing himself was enough, and the cat left, swearing blasphemies. Next morning it was discovered that the dancing epidemic had miraculously stopped. Thereupon the magistrates of the town decided that the best way to hunt down Satan was to burn live cats and the people believed that the ritual burnings which took place on the Eve of St. John commemorated their release from the epidemic. The annual celebration was led by the Governor and Municipal Magistrate who headed a procession of halberdiers and torch-bearers. They walked three times round the pile of faggots on top of which were the baskets of cats. The Governor and Magistrate then lit the fire and the crowd danced round. Not till 1773 did the wife of the Governor succeed in having the custom stopped. A similar procedure was followed at Melun in the district of Siene-et-Marne where the people afterwards collected the scraps of charcoal as charms against lightening. The last annual bonfire was held there on 12th June 1739.

The most completely Christianized version of the ceremony took place every year at Aix-en-Provence and was not discontinued until 1757. The finest tom-cat that could be found was wrapped in swaddling clothes like the infant Jesus and exhibited for adoration in an elaborate shrine. Flowers were strewn before his litter as he was taken in procession. But when the sun crossed the meridian at twelve noon on 24th June the cat was placed in a wicker basket and thrown alive onto a huge bonfire lit in the city square. This custom was fully approved by the Church bishops and priests who sang the anthem at the sacrifice; yet it is obvious that it preserved elements of pagan cults and sun-worship.

Other customs also point back to a pagan origin. At Ypres during the Middle Ages two or three cats were thrown from the cathedral belfry every second Sunday in May. Since this custom was carried out in the month of May and not varied with changes in the date of Easter it may be that the custom preserved a form of the belief that May was the time for ritual purification. In the old tradition only kittens born in May were considered unclean. Now being associated with pagan practices, and therefore evil, all cats could be candidates for destruction.

On Shrove Tuesday-eve at Store Magleby near Copenhagen a live cat was imprisoned in a barrel at which horsemen tilted, and in the English village of Albrighton a cat was whipped to death on Shrove Tuesday. This is commemorated in Albrighton's old inn sign which reads,

The finest passtime under the sun—is whipping the cat at Albrighton.

Inn signs of the 'Cat in the Basket' or the 'Cat in the Cage' probably commemorate a similar custom.

At Kelso in Roxburghshire a cat was put in a barrel half-filled with soot and slung between two high poles. It was then belaboured with staves till it fell apart and the half-crazed cat fell out and was killed by the crowd. An old Welsh custom celebrated at Dolgelly during the Assizes in August was to collect cats and release them on the marina to be hunted by dogs. This was regarded as an exciting part of the local festivities at least until 1784.

Although these sadistic practices, which were supposed to purge the community of the Devil's influence, no doubt appealed to many people there were some who evidently thought it would be simpler to keep on the right side of the Devil by treating his emissary, the cat, as a favoured member of the family. From the West of Ireland we learn that:

There was a woman had a cat and she would feed it at the table before any other one; and if it did not get the first meat that was cooked, the hair would rise up as high as that. Well, there were priests came to dinner one day, and when they were helped the first, the hair rose up on the cat's back. And one of them said to the woman it was a queer thing to give in to a cat the way she did, and that it was a foolish thing to be giving it the first food. So when it heard that, it walked out of the house, and never came into it again.

A more cautious person expressed the view that:

You should never be too attentive to a cat, but just to be civil and to give it its share.

W. B. Yeats has described what was believed to have happened to a cat which belonged to the father of a newspaper editor he knew. One day the priest dined with the old man and objected to seeing the cat fed before Christians. He made some comment and the cat sprang away up the chimney in 'a flame of fire'. Then said the editor's father:

'I will have the law on you for doing such a thing to my cat.'
'Would you like to see your cat?' said the priest.
'I would,' said he, and the priest brought it up, covered with chains, through the hearth-rug, straight from hell.

Yeats also recounted how a 'Demon Cat' stole fish and scratched people until it was burned up by holy water being poured over it.

It is widely believed that to ill-treat a cat brings bad luck. If a 'Cat-King' and rituals for securing his aid were still vaguely remembered by a society whose official religion condemned such practices it would be natural for superstitious people to feel that it was still worthwhile invoking the cat for 'luck'. In Europe the white cat is generally considered unlucky although in this next verse the black cat is unlucky:

> *Black cat, black cat—when he cross yo' track*
> *No matter whar you gwine,*
> *To a dippin' or a dyin'*
> *No matter whar you hurryin'*
> *To a marrying or a buryin'*
> *You better turn back.*

The Ozarks believed that to see a white cat on the road was lucky. In Cambridgeshire it is the unexpected sight of a black cat that is lucky. White cats also can bring good fortune if seen by chance, otherwise they herald bad news. Peter and Iona Opie, the acknowledged experts on the folk culture of children, have found that English school-children believe seeing a white cat on the way to school is sure to bring trouble. To avert bad luck they say one must either spit, or turn around completely and make the sign of the cross. Some say it is necessary to turn around three times. To meet a black cat is lucky but one must say 'black cat bring me luck' or stroke it three times from head to tail and make a wish. If the black cat is sitting on the path or if it walks ahead all will be well. But if it takes avoiding action, particularly if it crosses from left to right, it means very bad luck indeed.

A black cat in a house brings good luck but to steal a cat from a house is unlucky. The Irish say that when moving house one should either leave the cat behind or take it to the new home several days before the move. To the Ozarks a strange black cat visiting a home meant good luck but if it stayed, bad luck could be expected to follow. The reason given for this was that the cat had foreseen poverty or that rats and mice were likely to be plentiful. If a black cat enters a house in Sicily it is chased out at once to avert trouble because, it is said, it has 'the evil eye'.

Most people are interested in the sort of good luck which brings worldly wealth. Sir John Denham, a seventeenth-century poet wrote:

> *Kiss the black cat,*
> *And that'll bring ye fat:*
> *Kiss ye the white one*
> *And that'll make ye lean.*

As wealth was once thought to be incompatible with Christian morality, what better animal to assure riches than Satan's pet, the cat? There is an old saying that:

Them that ever mind the world to win
Must have a black cat, a howling dog and a crowing hen.

Parts of the cat's anatomy could be made into charms or potions for good fortune. In the *Masque of Queens* by Ben Jonson there are these lines:

> *I from the jaws of a gardener's bitch*
> *Did snatch these bones, and then leaped the ditch,*
> *Yet I went back to the house again,*
> *Killed the black cat, and here's the brain.*

A medieval belief was that if one wished always to be rich one must bury a cat with a gold coin, having first closed its eyes with two black beans. In the Lowlands of Brittany it is believed that in the fur of every black cat there is one pure white hair. If you can find this and pull it out without the cat scratching you, you will have a very powerful good-luck talisman. You may choose either business success or to be lucky in love. Today, people who would not go to this amount of trouble still carry black-cat lucky charms in their cars and on key-rings.

In Brittany there is a *chat d'argent*, a silver or money-cat, who can serve nine masters and make them all rich. The number nine, so often associated with cats, suggests that each of its 'lives' may be devoted to a different person. Throughout the Midi of France people believe in 'matagots' or magician-cats. They are black and have the power to attract wealth to the house where they are well fed and cared for. To catch a matagot you must lure it with a chicken and then grab it by the tail and carry it home in a sack without once looking backwards. Having got your matagot home, put it in a chest and always give it the first mouthful every time you eat. This will ensure that every morning you will find a gold coin at the bottom of the chest. Some Irish people also fed the cat first and their convictions may stem from the same source as the belief in matagots. People near Marseilles have long believed in matagots, and in Provence the nick-name 'Cost' or 'Cost-matagot' is given to people who are lucky. In Provence there is the conflicting opinion that it is unwise for a late traveller to answer any greeting after sunset in case it comes from a matagot, who is described as one who is 'too good for hell and not good enough for heaven', who manifests himself as a cat, and does mischief to humans. This suggests that matagots were derived from pagan beliefs and that Christians were discouraged from having anything to do with them.

'Puss in Boots' is the story of a typical matagot who enabled a poor boy to become rich. But the man best known for becoming rich with the help of a cat is, of course, Dick Whittington whose cat also had matagot characteristics. The link with matagots is emphasized by the tradition which persists that Whittington was a poor boy although in fact he was the third son of Sir William Whittington, Lord of the Manor of Pauntley in Gloucestershire.

Although the Church attempted to stamp out the older European religions and taught that the cat associated with them was a manifestation of the Devil, there are many stories of saints, such as St. Jerome, who kept a cat. He is frequently shown with a domestic cat instead of or as well as his lion, and the painting called *Saint Jerome in His Study* by Antonello de Messina has a very comfortable-looking cat in it. This little rhyme suggests that he was the only saint to own a cat but in fact many did:

> *If I lost my little cat, I should be sad without it,*
> *I should ask St. Jerome what to do about it,*
> *I should ask St. Jerome, just because of that*
> *He's the only Saint I know that kept a pussy-cat.*

Accounts of the early saints do not have a high claim to authenticity but they probably reflect a popular knowledge of, and sympathy with the practices which the stories reflect. Most of the saints' pets were innocent companions but in some cases a pagan tradition was Christianized by becoming attached to them, and in other cases it seems that a saint or his followers had fallen back into a pagan cult or had become attracted to the Manichaean heresy in which cats played a ritual part.

St. Gertrude cared for the souls of the dead which came to her as mice and in Italy there is a legend that St. Francis was saved from a plague of mice by a cat which sprang miraculously out of his sleeve. As St. Francis is known to have had Muslim contacts this story may be a variant of the story of the Prophet and his cat. St. Martha of the first century is said to have had a cat as a companion and in Sicily the cat is sacred to her and treated with respect: he who kills one will be unhappy for seven years. But Sicilians also regarded cats as having the 'evil eye' and thought that a cat which miaowed when boats were leaving harbour could influence the weather.

St. Agatha, who died in 251, is still known as Santo Gato (literally 'Saint Cat') in the old Province of Languedoc and in the Pyrenees Mountains. Languedoc later became the centre of the Albigensian Heresy, a sect of the Manichaeans who were accused of worshipping a cat. When angered by women working on her day, 5th February, St. Agatha appeared in the form of a cat to punish them. Weather predictions were traditionally made on this day and cats roaming in February, the month in which her day occurs, were regarded as witches. She could produce hail and thunderstorms and coupled with the fact that the Nine Priestesses of Sark, and later the witches, raised storms, Santo Gato may either have been connected with a pagan cult concerned with the weather or became the Christian embodiment of it.

John the Deacon in his *Life of Saint Gregory the Great* gives an account of a hermit who lived in the sixth century. A man of great saintliness, he possessed no worldly goods except a cat, which he constantly stroked and held in his arms. When he prayed to God to show him what place in heaven he might hope to occupy in reward for his holiness God appeared to him in a dream and told him that he could occupy the same place as Pope Gregory. This made the hermit feel that his renunciation of the world had been of little use if he was to share a place in heaven with a wealthy man like the Pope. But in a later dream God reproved him saying:

> Since a man is not rich by reason of what he owns, but of what he loves, how dare you compare your poverty with Gregory's wealth, when you can be convicted of showing more affection for that cat of yours, fondling it every day and sharing it with no one, than he does for all his riches, which he does not love, but lavishes on all?

The hermit accepted his reproof and prayed earnestly that he might indeed come to the same place in heaven as Pope Gregory. Experts differ as to whether the Latin text should translate that the cat was his 'house-mate' or 'lady friend' and John the Deacon does not tell us whether, after being admonished by God, the hermit stopped fondling his cat. Another ambiguity in the translation is a little suspicious: when God refers to the cat and accuses the hermit of 'sharing it with no one' the translation could equally well be 'not allowing that it can be compared with anyone' which, if taken in conjunction with the translation of the cat as his 'lady friend', makes it look as if the good hermit was engaged in some form of adoration of a goddess in the form of a cat.

The Welsh Prince Cado who became an anchorite and was later known as St. Cado is reputed to have given a cat to the Devil on a bridge. It was once generally believed that the difficult task of building a bridge could only be completed with help from the Devil. The fee demanded by him was usually the first person to cross, but he was often tricked by being given a cat which, it was said, must have been the first to cross on one of the many occasions when the Devil had been in cat-form himself (an explanation which can only date from the time when the Devil replaced the pagan deities to whom the cat had been sacred). The 'Ninth World' presided over by Freya was reached by a golden bridge and in pagan tradition the land of the living and the land of the dead were separated by a river over which souls crossed by a bridge. Rivers and their crossings would therefore seem terrifying and this would be sufficient reason not to offend any supernatural being when building a bridge.

Many bridges in Western Europe and the British Isles are still called 'The Devil's Bridge'. The Lord Mayor of Beaugency on the Loire promised the Devil the first to cross the fine new bridge being built across the river. When the bridge was completed he carried a cat to one end and, pouring a bucket of water over it, drove it across to the Devil. In Brittany a bishop gave the Devil a black cat when told that some peasants had contracted with the Devil for the first soul to cross a bridge in exchange for his help in building it. In France it is still regarded as unlucky to cross a stream with a cat in one's arms and a coat-of-arms consisting of a cat standing by a bridge probably illustrates this superstition.

At Dulverton in Somerset a natural stone bridge called Torr Steps crosses the River Barle. According to local tradition it was built in one night by the Devil who intended it for his own private use. To stop mortals crossing he announced that the first to trespass upon it would be destroyed. But the Devil was deceived again by a cat which was driven across. The next person to cross was the parson but the Devil honoured his promise and the bridge has been open to the public ever since. Ruth Tongue in 1963 collected this account of what happened from a Somersetshire drover:

> Then he [the cat] heard yells of rage and off he scuttles to see what 'twas and it were the Devil and Parson, one on each side of the Barle and a new stone bridge atween 'm. 'I'll have a look-see at that,' says Cat and down hill he goes.
>
> Says Parson to Devil, 'You shan't have none of my souls be first step on your bridge. They bain't goin' Somewhere Else.'
>
> 'You old black crow,' yells Devil.
>
> 'If I be a crow,' says Parson, 'I bain't so black as yew!'
>
> And just then puss walk out over onto Tarr Steps to look it over, no matter, if he'd invited or no. The Devil pounced on 'n like lightning flash—and poor Cat goed Somewhere Else quicker than you could think!

Very old traditions demand that a human sacrifice be placed in the foundations or the roof-tree of a new building. In 563 when St. Columba began to build the monastery of Iona, the work was hindered by 'spirits of the soil' who nightly undid what had been built during the day. He called for a volunteer and one of his disciples was interred in the foundations to propitiate them. In Ireland Clonmaclois Church was consecrated by the burial of a leper who was one of St. Patrick's followers.

Later, a cat was substituted for the human sacrifice. Their skeletons are often found when medieval buildings are being restored or altered. The shrivelled corpse of a cat, said to have come from between the walls of Westminster Abbey when the east end was being rebuilt, was displayed at a coffee house in Chelsea during the eighteenth century. Other remains of sacrificial cats have been found, including one in a house built by Sir Christopher Wren between 1666 and 1723 in the precincts of the Tower of London. Another was sealed into a passage under the roof of the Wren church, St. Michael Royal. This passage had never been opened so the cat must have been placed there by Wren's workmen when the church was built in 1687. Perhaps the horrors of the plague followed by the destruction caused by the Fire of London tempted people to revive old superstitious customs connected with the preservation of buildings which had been in abeyance for a long time.

10

Another beginning in India

See, the arched back, the tail erected, stiff,
Bent at the tip and twisting, and the ear
Flat to the head, and the eye quick with fear
Darting a single glance, debating if
The way to get inside the house is clear:
And on the other side, its gullet fat
With panting, growling, hoarse with its own breath,
With sneering lips that lift to show its teeth,
And slavering jaws, the dog attacks the cat.

(Sanskrit poem by YOGEŚVARA)

In order to understand the significance of many of the stories which form part of our literary and pre-literate inheritance we must turn back in time to early beginnings. Not this time to Egypt but to India. The cat as a cult object and a religious symbol derived from Egypt. On the other hand, with very few exceptions all European languages are derived from an Indo-European root language, an early form of which developed in India. Therefore, tales which have survived in India reflect the traditions of Aryan peoples who carried them with them in their migrations and are now found wherever Indo-European languages are spoken.

In approximately 2000 B.C. at the town called Chanhu-daro on the river Indus a dog chased a cat across newly made bricks laid out to dry in the sun. They left their footprints on the soft clay, the paw of the dog slightly overlaying that of the cat. When the bricks were fired the paw marks were preserved, to be revealed again when Chanhu-daro, which had been destroyed by invading Aryan hordes, was excavated in this century. So when the Aryans, those first speakers of an Indo-European language, rode into India from the north soon after 2000 B.C. the cat was there, ready and waiting to rub round their legs as soon as they got out of their chariots.

Therefore, in the myths of Aryan India it is not surprising that cats occur in association with other animals whose shared characteristics made them suitable symbols of the same idea. The hedgehog and the mongoose hunt snakes; weasels and cats hunt small vermin, and ants are industrious scavengers. Thus these animals are aggressive hunters on their own account and at the same time they act as natural protectors of man's interests on farms and in villages and small towns. They can, therefore, all be thought of as two-faced: treacherous adversaries to their enemies and vigilantes in man's environs.

Because everyone could understand the practical role of these animals in relation to man they were used by the story-teller and myth-maker to present abstract or religious ideas. The myths form a sequence which can be traced back to the Rigvedas, the earliest Aryan poetic works which were composed about 1500 B.C. The most ancient are about ants and a little later in the series there are tales of hedgehogs, then mongooses and weasels, and the most recent ones are about cats. In these stories the animal behaves according to its character as observed and understood in the practical realm by the hearer, but it carries out a magical or supernatural task. From being a practical aid and scavenger in the village it becomes a symbolic protector.

The danger from which man was protected symbolically by these animals was the night: the fear, very real for early man, that the sun would not return to the world. The acts they performed symbolically ensured that a new day would dawn and their stories explained this cosmic event in everyday terms. The cat, the weasel, the mongoose and also mice, moles, serpents and ants are all either stealthy and quiet or keep themselves hidden. This makes them good symbols of night. Mice, moles and serpents form a group which hide when not foraging for food, but the other group, the cats, weasels and mongooses can be stealthy thieves as well as stealthy hunters of the first group of thieving animals. Thus this second group become symbolic protectors against the dangers that lurk in the night, and since the moon illuminates the night, these animals are identified with the moon.

In one of the Rigvedas, Indra takes the form of an ant to fight and drive away the serpent-monster who invades the skies and causes darkness. In later tales the morning and evening heavens are compared to granaries. During the night ants separate the grain from the chaff, purify it of all that is unclean and transport it from west to east: which is to say they cleanse the sky of nocturnal shadows. In the course of time these ant stories were replaced by stories of the hedgehog and the mongoose, both of which hunt snakes. In a later version of the Rigveda tale it is Indra as a hedgehog, not an ant, who defeats the serpent of the sky. It is interesting that the Roman historian Pliny tells of ants in India being as big as foxes and the colour of cats. As there are Indian tales of monster ants perhaps he mistook a mythical story for a description of fact.

The word in Sanskrit (the oldest surviving Indo-European language) for mongoose is *Nakulas* which means 'destroyer'. It is the enemy and destroyer of mice and snakes and mythically it destroys the serpent of night. The Egyptians worshipped the mongoose, which they sometimes referred to as 'Pharoah's Cat', at the city of Herakliopolis and they believed that the Sun-God Ra symbolized by a cat killed the evil snake of darkness. In the course of time in India and Egypt the mongoose was replaced by the cat for vermin control, as were the weasel-like animals in Europe. When this happened stories which had been about the hedgehog, mongoose or weasel were retold with the cat as protagonist. This would have been natural and indeed necessary if the stories were to continue to have meaning for their hearers. As with religious belief, and these stories were originally religious myths, they had either to remain relevant or disappear.

The earliest preserved Indian book in which stories specifically about cats occur is the *Mahâbharata*, a great compendium of religion, myth and fable compiled over a long period between 400 B.C. and A.D. 400. Some of the pieces in it may have first appeared in other earlier Indian books of the seventh and eighth centuries B.C. but these are now lost.

The story of 'The Cat and the Mouse' tells how a cat and a

mouse lived in the same jungle tree, the cat among the branches eating small birds and the mouse, which had so far kept clear of the cat's paws, in a hole among the roots. One night a hunter placed a net beneath the tree and caught the cat in its meshes. The mouse, delighted at the cat's misfortune, tauntingly walked round the trap, nibbling the bait and generally making the most of the cat's bad luck. But suddenly it became aware of two new enemies, an owl overhead and a mongoose stalking through the undergrowth. Instantly the mouse promised to bite through the meshes of the net and release the cat if in return the cat would allow it to take refuge in the trap. The cat agreed and the mouse slipped quickly in. Feeling secure again the mouse was in no hurry to release its natural enemy, and saying it would wait till the hunter returned, subjected the cat to the indignity of having the mouse take a nap hidden in its fur. At the very last moment, as the hunter approached, the mouse quickly gnawed through the net and darted into its hole while the cat made a leap for the safety of the branches.

A cat caught in a net and liberated by mice biting through the threads is a common theme in Indian folk tales. It reminds us of the world-wide and ancient game of 'Cat's Cradle'. This is thought to have originated either from a desire to enmesh the setting sun and ensure by means of sympathetic magical ritual that it would return in the morning, or from a belief that at night the sun is caught in a trap from which it must be released by the 'grey mice of the night' nibbling through the meshes of its trap. The 'cat's cradle' and the cat caught in a net are clearly similar figures of poetic imagery. If the moon was thought of as replacing the sun during the night and if the cat was the symbol of the moon, it follows that the cat would also by proxy be the symbol of the absent sun. We have seen already that the Egyptians also thought of the cat as a symbol of both the sun and the moon.

In a hymn from the Rigvedas there is the saying: 'Mice tear their tails by gnawing them'. It is now thought that this should translate: 'Mice tear their threads by gnawing them'. If this is so then the grey mice of night, by biting through the threads of the trap, would be liberating the sun.

Another beginning in India

In myths about the protecting role of the moon it is the white cat that symbolizes the silvery moon prying into corners, dispersing the shadows of night and cleansing the sky ready for the day to follow. This white cat is the 'cleaner' or 'the animal that cleans itself' described by the Sanskrit word *Mârgâras*. This word is very similar to *Mârgaras* which means 'the hunter, the investigator, or one who follows the track'. In this sense the road or track is understood to be in contrast to the forest which is trackless and dark. This makes the white cat the cleaner or the killer of the forces that lurk in darkness. The most direct identification of the cat with the moon is to be found in these lines from Sanskrit poems where the poetic elements moon, milk and cat are assimilated to each other by the simplest and oldest of devices —they are literally incorporated by swallowing:

> *The cat laps the moon-beams in the bowl of water,*
> *Thinking them to be milk.*

> *A ray is caught in a bowl,*
> *And the cat licks it, thinking that it's milk.*

> *Look at the cloud-cat, lapping there on high*
> *With lightning tongue the moon milk from the sky.*

If the white cat is the cleanser of shadows and a protector from the dangers which lurk in the dark, then *Aranyamarguarus* is the treacherous black cat of the dark moonless night symbolized by the trackless forest. In India a black cat is still considered bad luck although in Europe the roles are often reversed and the white cat is unlucky.

The unpredictable nature of the cat or, rather, the uncertainty of the moon which the cat symbolizes, are the themes of two Indian stories known as 'The Penitent Cat' and 'Butter Ears'. The story of 'The Penitent Cat' comes from the *Mahâbharata* and finds a place on the rock sculpture of 'The Descent of the Ganges' at Mamallapuram near Madras. This huge carving represents the entire creation from devas in the sky through holy-men down to the animal kingdom giving thanks to Siva for his gift of the waters of the Ganges from the Himalayas. The 'Penitent Cat' is shown

standing with its front paws above its head in the attitude of a
holy-man practising austerities while the mice look on in awe and
admiration. The story is that the cat, by seeming to be so devout,
gathers the mice around him so that he can easily catch them and
grow fat. The Code of Manus, a collection of Indian law compiled
in 325 B.C., about the time Alexander the Great invaded North
India, refers to this story when it says:

> Let no man, apprised of this law, present even water to a
> priest who acts like a cat.

'Butter Ears' is one of the tales in the *Pancatantrum*, an Indian
book of fables. Like the Penitent Cat, 'Butter Ears' pretends to be
a reformed character. He is called upon to act as judge in a dispute
between a duck (or in some versions a sparrow) and a hare.
Feigning deafness he lures them to come nearer so that he can hear
what they have to say and, of course, catches and eats them both.

An Indian court tale tells of a cat who went to heaven: a
Penitent and a Brahmin were competing in virtuosity at the
King's palace. Although it was known to be impossible for a
mortal, the Brahmin succeeded in going to one of the seven
heavens and returning with a flower that grew there. The
Penitent responded by saying that even his cat could do that. He
whispered in its ear and to the consternation of the court the cat
disappeared into the clouds. But one of the goddesses was so
enraptured by the cat that she would not let it return. The cat
explained that his master, the Penitent, was relying on his bringing back a heavenly flower, but the best that could be arranged
was for the cat to return to the world after a few centuries. The
court patiently waited for three centuries through which, by
the power of his goodness, the Penitent prevented their feeling the
effects of old age. At the end of this time 'the sky suddenly became
brilliant, and in the cloud of a thousand colours' the cat appeared,
enthroned.

Although this is apparently a sophisticated tale told at court it
contains the elements of a much older mythic account of the sun's
absence during the night. The cat finally reappears in all its glory
as does the sun at dawn.

Another beginning in India

The fear that the sun might not return at dawn and disquiet at the uncertain and changing nature of the moon, gave rise to a group of myths and stories intended by analogy with familiar animals and their habits to allay men's fears and make the mysterious universe more comprehensible. These stories of cosmic processes enacted on an everyday scale have spread and become firmly rooted in the story-telling of all Europe. In India the animals in these stories were at first ants and then mongooses, hedgehogs, and finally weasels and cats. In Europe where ants are not conspicuous and mongooses do not occur the stories were restricted to weasels and cats.

It will be remembered that the cat and the weasel were confused in Irish folk-lore and legend. The Danaan cats were said to be weasels and the Irish believed that both cats and weasels were fairies in animal form. Some regarded seeing a weasel on the road as good luck, and others thought it bad luck. They had the same mixed feelings about cats. The folk-lorist, Sean O Suilleabhain, tells us that 'the noble little woman' is the epithet used to avoid mentioning weasels at sea and we already know that it is forbidden to talk about cats when at sea. A most curious fact is that weasels do not occur in Ireland so that sayings about them must refer to another small carnivore such as the polecat or stone marten which, as in Greek, were originally all called by the same name. These remnants, which are still to be found in the European country most distant from India, indicate that myths about a weasel-like animal were taken to every corner of Europe by Aryan Indo-European language speakers at a very early date.

We have seen already that the cat gradually replaced the weasel as a vermin catcher in Greece and that this change was paralleled by stories which had at first been about the weasel being retold with the cat as the chief character.

This transition is illustrated by 'The Legend of Galanthis (how she helped her mistress and for doing so was changed into a cat)' told by Ovid in the Ninth Book of the *Metamorphoses*. The Goddess Lucinia is sitting cross-legged and with fingers interlocked to stay the birth of Hercules, when the maid 'Galanthis with hair of reddish hue ... as she was passing in and out of the house ...

saw the goddess seated on the altar holding her clinched hands upon her knees, and said to her: "Whoever you are, congratulate our mistress: Argive Alcmena is relieved; her prayers are answered and her child is born". Up leaped the goddess of birth, unclinching her hands and spread them wide in consternation; my bonds were loosed and I was delivered of my child. They said that Galanthis laughed in derision of the cheated deity. And as she laughed the cruel goddess caught her by the hair and dragged her on the ground; and, as the girl strove to rise, she kept her there and changed her arms into the forelegs of an animal. Her old activity remained and her hair kept its former hue; but her former shape was changed. And because she had helped her labouring mistress with her deceitful lips, through her mouth must she bring forth her young. And still, as of yore, she makes our dwelling place her home.'

To this day in Greece a deceitful woman is called a 'weasel', and according to William Smith in *A Classical Dictionary* it is uncertain whether Galanthis was changed into a cat or a weasel. This reflects the problem of the translation of the Greek word *gallê* but it also indicates that from a mythic point of view the weasel and the cat were regarded as similar. His account adds that Hecate took pity on Galanthis and took her as her attendant, which is one explanation of why the cat is associated with Hecate.

Lucinia, as her name indicates, was a moon-goddess and the cat or weasel into which Galanthis was changed were, as has been shown, both symbols of the moon. In this tale Ovid used very old folk traditions which refer back to a time when the moon was worshipped for its power to reveal the secrets of the night. The night represented the womb, and Hercules' difficult birth corresponded to the imagined difficulties of bringing forth each new day which in the minds of the ancients involved the same hazards and uncertainties as childbirth.

'The Penitent Cat' and 'Butter Ears' are both late Indian inventions only tenuously connected to the moon-myth from which they derive, but they are clearly destroyers. Also, in Sanskrit the moon can be called by a word meaning 'King of the

Forest Animals'. In Greek and Roman mythology Artemis and Diana are the Goddesses of Hunting and Forests. The symbol of Artemis, with which she is shown on Greek coins, is the moon and both Artemis and Diana were notorious for sometimes helping and sometimes destroying their followers. This is explained if originally they were personifications of the treacherous moon which sometimes bathed the earth in its gentle light and at other times left mankind in frightening darkness.

According to late Greek mythology the moon created the cat. Ovid recounts how Diana once disguised herself as a cat and Aesop used the old mythic material for his fable called 'Metamorphosis'.

A cat was enamoured of a handsome youth and begged Aphrodite to change her into a woman. The goddess, pitying her sad state, transformed her into a beautiful girl, and when the young man saw her he fell in love with her and took her home to be his wife. While they were resting in their bedroom, Aphrodite, who was curious to know if the cat's instincts had changed along with her shape, let a mouse loose in front of her. She at once forgot where she was, leapt up from the bed, and ran after the mouse to eat it. The indignant goddess then restored her to her original form.

Throughout Europe there are many proverbs which link the cat symbolically with the dual nature of the moon.

All cats are grey in the dark

implies that one cannot distinguish friend from foe in the anonymity of the night. The moon may be a guarantee of safety, a substitute sun and a reminder and promise of its return at dawn; or since the moon waxes and wanes, a dark moonless night can make man believe that the moon has behaved treacherously. When the slender black cat reclining on a silver couch gave vituperative answers in Connaught, Ireland (p. 94) it was this two-sided treacherousness of the moon that was being portrayed. The silver couch was the silvery moon and the black cat was the dark moonless night.

When the cat's away, the mice can play

is an ordinary enough proverb for a farming community, but it also warns that on moonless nights the forces of darkness can do as they please. Similarly the proverb which says:

The cat-moon eats the grey mice of night

describes what happens when the moon returns. The most apt description of the moon's cycle is given by the saying:

Curiosity killed the cat,
Satisfaction brought it back!

When the cat goes off to search out the dangers lurking in the night and does not return there is a dark moonless night: curiosity has killed the cat. When the new moon reappears in the sky it has been successful in its fight with the forces of darkness: satisfaction has brought it back.

In the Sanskrit language the epithet *Naktacarin* is applied both to a cat and to a thief. Before long the deceitful nature of the cat itself is more important than the original idea of using the deceptiveness of the cat as a symbol for the moon. As we saw in the case of the cat's changing eyes, once this happens the way is open for all sorts of magical beliefs and superstitions. There is a Hungarian belief that for a cat to be a good hunter it must itself have been stolen. It is as if even the owner of the cat must partake of the treachery associated with its nature if it is to perform well. The proverb

A borrowed cat catches no mice

continues the same trend of thought. More magical but still following the same idea is the 'Thieving Magic' from South Slavonia collected by Sir James Frazer and discussed in Chapter 3. Again it seems that when the mythical 'reason' for a belief was forgotten the cat was devalued from a symbol of the treacherous night to being a charm to aid a thief.

The other magical use of the cat in effecting the alternation of day and night is that embodied in the idea of a cat caught in a net, or a cat's cradle from which the grey mice of the night liberate it by biting through the threads. A faint echo of this idea finds expression in the nursery rhyme:

> *Some little mice sat in a barn to spin;*
> *Pussy came by, and popped her head in;*
> *'Shall I come in and cut your threads off?'*
> *'Oh no, kind Sir, you will snap our heads off!'*

By now the mythic quality of the tale has been lost and it is the cat who is threatening to bite off the threads for the mice which, once the symbolism had been forgotten, made more sense.

In Scotland, there is a belief that when a cat purrs it is saying 'threids and thrums' (threads and thread ends). The second verse of 'Willie Winkie' written by the Scottish poet William Miller in the nineteenth century goes:

> *Hey, Willie Winkie, are ye coming ben?*
> *The cat's singing grey thrums to the sleeping hen,*
> *The dogs spelder'd on the floor, and disna gie a cheep,*
> *But here's a waukrife laddie, that winna fa' asleep.**

The cat 'singing grey thrums' links the cat with threads and evokes in our minds an image of the quiet watchful cat as all nature, except Willie, sleeps. It is tempting to suggest that a Greek vase painting which shows two women playing with a cat and a bird and what seem to be balls of yarn may be enacting a ritual connecting cats with spun wool. The vase found in South Italy has been tentatively dated fifth century B.C. but the circumstances of its discovery are not certain. The Greek Fates known as Cataclothes or Greek Spinners may also be connected with the same constellation of beliefs.

Thus we see that in the traditions of Indo-European speakers the cat as a symbol of the moon and its mythic counterpart the moonless night has been used in an attempt to make the potential dangers of the alternation of day and night less fearful. Over the centuries these stories have been told and retold, adapted for the different tastes of villagers and courtiers and slowly spread across frontiers from India to the West of Ireland. There has been plenty

* ben = in, spelder'd = stretched, waukrife = wakeful.

of scope for changes and alterations to take place. But story-tellers stick tenaciously to essential details of a tradition and as we shall see in the next chapter the same basic elements can still be found.

11

A fairy-tale cat

A basin of water she took,
  And dashed in poor Catskin's face;
But briskly her ears she shook,
  And went to her hiding place,
        . . . .
In a rage the ladle she took,
  And broke poor Catskin's head;
But off she went shaking her ears,
  And swift to her forest she fled.
        . . . .
In a fury she took the skimmer,
  And broke poor Catskin's head;
But heart-whole and lively as ever,
  Away to her forest she fled.
                    (*Traditional*)

The 'fairy tales' of Europe preserve many tales in which the identification of the cat with the moon is still to be found. This reveals that they were once myths, stories about supernatural characters and events held in common by all Indo-European-language speaking peoples. Fairy tales in this sense are not stories about fairies but orally-transmitted folk-tales such as those collected by the brothers Grimm, and more sophisticated tales by known authors but based upon folk traditions such as the 'Mother Goose' tales written by Charles Perrault in the seventeenth century. In these tales the fortunes of the hero or heroine depend to some degree upon magical intervention or enchantment. Those which deal with the cat-moon myth reveal themselves as sharing the following characteristics. The tale may be set in a dark forest, a lonely castle or within some enclosed space which symbolizes the night. A cat may help a seemingly disadvantaged person to complete an impossible task or to right some injustice. The heroine may be disguised as a cat. There is a marriage or reunion of the two principal characters who are often a prince and princess, or a poor boy and a princess. Magical objects such as an endless piece of coloured cloth, a gold ring, or a magical animal, all of which are symbols of the sun, are used.

'Cat-Skin' is the name of the German version of the fairy-tale 'Cinderella' collected by the brothers Grimm in the early nineteenth century. It begins by describing a queen with hair of purest gold, who was the most beautiful woman in the world. Unhappily she fell ill and died after making her husband, the king, promise that he would not remarry unless he could find a bride as beautiful as herself. This he could not do: only the daughter was as beautiful as the mother. At last the king thought that perhaps he could marry his daughter, but she and all the courtiers were very shocked at this suggestion. Hoping to make the king give up the idea of marrying her, the daughter said: 'Before I marry anyone I must have three dresses; one is to be of gold like the sun, another of shining silver like the moon, and a third as dazzling as the stars: besides this, I want a mantle of a thousand different kinds of fur, to which every beast in the kingdom must give a part of its skin.'

Undeterred by these conditions, the king ordered his most skilful tailors to make the three dresses and the cloak. When they were ready he presented them to the princess. That night she arose when all the palace slept, packed the three dresses in a nut-shell with a ring, a necklace and a brooch all made of gold, blackened her face and hands and, wrapped in the cloak of fur, left the palace.

After travelling a long way she came to a forest where she rested in a hollow tree. The next day she was found by huntsmen out with their master, the king of a neighbouring country. 'I am a poor child that has neither father nor mother left; have pity on me and take me with you,' she said. 'Yes Miss Cat-Skin,' they said, 'You will do for the kitchen; you can sweep up the ashes and things of that sort.'

For a long time she worked as a kitchen maid. Then the king decided to hold a ball. When all the guests had arrived Cat-Skin asked the cook if she might go up and stand behind the door of the great hall to peep in at the dancing. 'Yes, you may go, but be back again in half an hour's time to rake out the ashes,' said the cook.

Cat-Skin hurried to her little room, washed off the soot and put on one of her beautiful dresses. When she entered the hall everyone thought she must be a strange princess. She was so beautiful that the king danced with her. Afterwards she slipped away without being seen, went to her room, removed the dress, blackened her hands and face and put on her fur cloak again. She returned to the kitchen where the cook told her to make some soup for the king. This she did very nicely and put her gold ring in the bottom of the bowl. The king thought the soup was the best he had ever tasted and when he got to the bottom of the bowl he found the ring. The cook, when sent for, told him that Cat-Skin had prepared the soup. Then Cat-Skin was sent for and the king asked her who she was, but she denied all knowledge of the ring and said that she was only fit to have the boots and shoes thrown at her head.

After a while the king held another ball. Events followed the same pattern and the king found a gold brooch at the bottom of the soup bowl. A third ball was given, and this time while Cat-Skin and the king were dancing he managed to slip a ring onto her finger without her noticing. Later, she made his soup as before and put her gold necklace in the bowl. But her dance with the king had gone on for so long that she had not had time to blacken her hands properly. One finger was left white and she had not removed her beautiful dress but put the fur cloak on over it. When the king sent for her he at once saw his ring on the unblackened finger. As he took her hand she tried to pull away and a corner of the lovely dress showed under the cape.

At last the king had discovered who his beautiful princess was and they were married, never to part.

Relating this well-known fairy-tale to the myths in which a cat represented the moon it becomes apparent that when the princess wears her glittering dresses she is the resplendent full moon. When she dons her cloak she is the hidden, waned moon. The forest that she travels through is the night, and when she is eventually married with the king, who is the sun, the necessary balance between day and night, which is the reason for the myth, is established.

Apart from the girl's nickname no cat is mentioned in the tale, although when Cat-Skin says she is only fit to have the boots and shoes thrown at her head she is identifying herself with the moon's symbol, the cat, at which boots and shoes are often thrown. That she can slip out of the ballroom without being missed is also very cat-like. In the long English poem called 'Catskin', part of which is quoted at the head of this chapter and which tells the same story, the cook's actions show unmistakably the identity of cat and girl although no cat is directly mentioned in this poem either.

That Cat-Skin is always employed at the hearth links her with the idea of a 'hearth goddess' such as the Roman Goddess Vesta who guarded the sacred temple-fire and whose name is a latinized form of Diana. To guard a fire, especially a sacred fire, is symbolically very much the same thing as to ensure the safety of the sun: since cats are very often found at the hearth-side they are doubly suited to this role.

There is another cat-moon who guards a fire. It is in a grey monochrome painting called *Death of the Virgin*, by Pieter Brueghel the Elder. On the right-hand side of the picture the Virgin lies in her bed suffused by an unearthly light and surrounded by a group of people. The only other light in the painting is from a fire-place on the left. In front of it, fully illuminated and set off by the empty picture space around it, sits a cat. The painting gives an impression of great mystery but no one seems to have commented on the cat or its significance in the painting. Can it be that Brueghel was responding to an unconscious need to have the moon's representative keep vigil while the 'Queen of Heaven' died?

In Aesop's fable of 'The Cat and the Fox' the fox, a predator and thief in the night is tricked and killed. In a Russian version of the same tale the cat marries the fox and they combine to terrify other forest animals which symbolize the dangers of the night-forest.

A fairy-tale cat

The most sophisticated form of this story-type is the French fairy tale 'Reynard the Fox'. The earliest version which has come down to us is a court story of the tenth century but elements of it must have existed in folk tradition for a very long while before then. The cat, Tybert, is sent to fetch Reynard to court to account for his misdeeds. Tybert arrives at the fox's lair but that night Reynard tricks him into entering the priest's barn where there are mice to catch. Reynard does not tell him that the priest has set a trap, in which Tybert is promptly caught. Hearing the commotion which Tybert makes, the priest jumps out of bed, runs naked into the barn and begins to beat the trapped cat. As illustrated in the Bristol Cathedral carvings Tybert makes a desperate bid for freedom and in the process almost castrates the priest.

> *C'en est fait de nos amours !*
> *Je suis veuve sans recours !*

laments his wife. This gave rise to the saying quoted by John Skelton in the early sixteenth century.

> A peryllous thynge, to cast a cat
> Vpon a naked man and yf she scrat.

Tybert returns to the court and relates his misfortunes at the hands of the priest and the fox. The king confers with his councillors on how Reynard is to be brought to justice but when the fox comes to court he is well treated because he is able to show that the other animals had been conspiring to kill the king.

That this tale derives from a very old tradition is revealed by the veiled allusion to a cat-moon protagonist against a forest animal which represents the darkness of night. The version which we have is from a later period when the original theme had been reversed and the fox and the priest combine to trick the cat. This alteration made it possible to continue telling the tale long after moon worship had been replaced by Christianity. Clawing the priest is Tybert's only victory.

There is a Russian tale about a poor boy who buys a cat, a dog and a magic ring. The magic ring enables the boy to marry a king's daughter, but she is deceitful and only wants the ring. She gets the boy drunk, steals the ring and departs to live in a castle in a remote part of the country. The dog and cat set out to recover the ring for their master. When they reach the castle they take employment there and the cat catches a mouse with whom it makes a bargain. The princess sleeps with the ring in her mouth, and in return for its life the mouse is to dangle its tail in her mouth. When the mouse does this the princess spits out the ring. The cat and dog return with it to the boy who uses it to force the princess to come back to him. Here the sun is symbolized both by the magic ring and by the princess who goes away to a distant place, as the sun was thought to do during the night. The story makes the sun doubly out of sight since at night it is also concealed as the ring within the mouth of the princess. The cat is the moon who, with the help of that shadowy creature of the night, the mouse, brings the sun, in the form of the princess and the magic ring, back to the world of men, symbolized by the boy.

Another Russian story is about the youngest of three sisters who is married to a prince and has three sons. Her jealous sisters make the prince believe that she has given birth to a cat, a dog and a 'vulgar child'. Her real sons are taken away and she is blinded, encased in a barrel with the 'vulgar child' and thrown into the sea. Later, the barrel is washed up on the shore and splits open. The child bathes the mother's eyes and her sight is restored. From this point there are two versions of events. In one the princess finds her three sons who have become luminous and light everything near with their splendour. In the other version the mother and the child take refuge on an island where, perched on a pillar of gold, sits a cat who sings songs and tells tales. When the mother finds her three real sons they are handsome youths with legs of silver, chests of gold and foreheads like the moon. In both accounts she is then re-united with her husband, the prince. Here again is the same symbolic pattern. The moon's light wanes and is extinguished as the mother is discredited, blinded and cast away in a barrel. One of the offsprings she is said to have produced is a cat. When the barrel has burst open and her sight is restored, a cat sits on a gold pillar: the moon is again waxing. Her three sons either project the effect of moonlight on all around them, or combine the sun and the moon in their bodies. She is reunited with the prince and all is well with the world.

Also from Russia comes the tale of a cat who shows a girl how to escape from a witch. The cat gives the girl a magic towel which, when thrown down, causes a river to appear, and a magic comb which can cause an impenetrable forest to grow. By these means the girl is able to prevent the witch from following her. Here the girl is the dawn escaping the clutches of the night-witch, who is kept from pursuit by the dark forest of night and by the river which divides day from night. In the story about the Danaans, the ancient inhabitants of Ireland, an enchanted cat guarded a magic comb. When the old man combed his hair with it, his youth, the morning of life, was restored to him. We can see now that this comb guarded by a cat was of the same kind as was used mythically to cleanse the night-sky of its shadows. It links together Indian and Celtic mythology with later fairy tales.

Another group of fairy tales concerns a cat which comes to the rescue of a cock, symbol of the new day. In one account the cock, while searching for the bark of trees, is caught three times by a fox and rescued each time by the cat. That the cock is searching for bark seems to suggest that it is in the night-forest when the fox, a nocturnal animal, catches it. The cat-moon rescues the cock so that it can perform its traditional role as herald of each new day.

> *The cat walks upon its feet*
> *In red boots;*
> *It wears a sword by its side,*
> *And a stick by its thigh;*
> *It wishes to kill the fox,*
> *And to make its soul perish.*

So sings the cat as it rescues the cock from the fox in a more dramatic rendering of the tale. The fox and his seven, or in another variant, five daughters have imprisoned the cock in their den. One at a time the daughters and finally the fox, are lured out and killed. The number of daughters may refer to the days of the week which emphasizes the fact that the drama must be enacted every night to liberate the cock for each new dawn.

The red boots of the cat symbolize the sunrise and a cat wearing red boots immediately brings to mind 'Puss in Boots', that swash-buckling cat who by a series of audacious tricks made a fortune for the poor boy who was his owner. 'Puss in Boots' is one of eight tales published by Charles Perrault as *The Tales of Mother Goose* in the seventeenth century. A picture of an old woman spinning as she tells tales to a group consisting of a man, a girl and a boy and a cat, formed an evocative frontispiece to the first edition.

We have already seen (p. 108) that Puss in Boots was a matagot cat. His deceitfulness is felt to be pardonable because it results in gain to the poor at the expense of the 'rich. Although a materialistic interpretation suited seventeenth-century readers, just enough clues to an earlier meaning remain. Using the analogy of the 'cat as helper' as in the previous stories, the youth's father who died is the setting sun, and the cat is the moon as helper through the dark night or time of poverty. The splendour of the new day is assured when the father's son is established in wealth with his beautiful bride.

The seventeenth-century tale *La Chatte Blanche* by Madame d'Aulnoy tells of a white cat named Blanchette who lives, veiled in black, in an enchanted palace. A prince comes riding on a wooden horse which mythically represents the journey into the dark forest of night. Blanchette gives him a tiny dog in an acorn. It is so small that it can pass through a ring. Next she gives him a marvellously-painted cloth enclosed in a grain of millet, and of such fine silk that it can pass through the eye of a needle. The acorn, the grain of millet and the eye of the needle all represent the sun, and the marvellously-coloured cloth is the sunrise. Finally, this wonderful cat, Blanchette, becomes a beautiful maiden with long golden hair. So the white cat of the night is replaced by the golden sunrise. But before this transformation takes place, the white cat asks the prince to help in a battle against some mice—the grey mice of the night.

Madame d'Aulnoy's tale is a sophisticated composition, but there exist other versions of it, some of which must be very old. One of these is 'The Story of the Piece of Cloth', a French tale from Upper Poitou about a king's three sons who all want to marry the same girl. The king sets them tasks to determine who shall be the bridegroom. They are to find the largest piece of cloth, the finest hunting dog and the prettiest girl. The youngest son, who is considered stupid, rides off, not thinking that he has any chance of winning the contest. He finds an enchanted castle in which lives a cat who helps him. First she gives him a tailor's box in which is an endlessly long piece of cloth with no seam in it. Then she gives him an egg in which there is a tiny green hunting dog which outruns all the other dogs brought back by his brothers. Finally when he goes to the cat for help in finding the prettiest girl, the cat lays its head down on the hearth and requests that he chop it off with one blow. The head flies into the fire and there instead of the cat is a beautiful girl dressed in a gown of gold and silver. They ride together to the father's castle and the king is forced to agree that this son has won all the contests. But now the boy wants to marry his enchanted cat and they return together to her castle.

Versions of this tale have also been collected from many parts of Ireland. Sometimes the three young men are described as farmers' sons, but one of the tasks is always to find the most beautiful girl and she is revealed when the cat is beheaded or burned to death.

The youngest son represents the sun. His finding the enchanted castle corresponds to the sun entering the night. This enchanted castle is described as being quite empty with only a cat, the moon-cat, moving about in it. An enchanted castle in fairy tale is always on a mountain top or in a gloomy forest. It may be the home of a good fairy, a magician, a witch, or simply the home of cats. In a Tuscan fairy tale cats living in an isolated place help a poor woman who has many children. She goes to their enchanted palace on the top of a mountain and cleans and cooks for them.

She encounters their king and asks him for alms. When told that she has treated his subjects well her apron is filled with gold coins. Her wicked sister then tries her luck on the mountain but she maltreats the cats and returns home scratched and terrified.

An Irish version of this tale has been collected by W. B. Yeats. It concerns two cousins, one kind-hearted, the other mean and cruel. In a rage the cruel cousin blinds the kind one and abandons him under a tombstone in a burial ground on a bleak hilltop. Soon a great miaowing is heard as if all the cats in the world were assembling on the hilltop. He hears them say that the king has been struck with blindness and has promised the hand of his daughter in marriage to the one who can restore his sight. The cats also add that the only cure is water from a certain well. When the cats have gone he manages to crawl to the well and heal himself. Returning home he tricks his cousin into going to the hilltop where the cats tear him to pieces. After further adventures the good cousin manages to fill a bottle with water from the well and go to the king's court. He cures the king's blindness, answers a riddle asked by the princess and marries her.

A charming Breton folk-tale called 'The Purr' is about the ambivalent, threatening-protecting aspects of the moon which are represented by three pure white cats and their playthings, balls of gold and linen thread. A king and queen who had long wanted a child finally had a daughter. But they were warned by a sorceress that their daughter would die if she ever gave her hand in marriage to a prince. 'Heed this advice. Find three pure white cats and let them grow up with your child. Give them balls of two types to play with—balls of gold and balls of linen thread. If they ignore the gold and play with the linen, all will be well, but if they ignore the linen and play with the gold, beware!'

The princess grew up with her three cats who always played with the linen balls so that the original purpose of the gold ones was almost forgotten. When the princess was sixteen and very beautiful many princes sought her hand in marriage, but she remained content to live with her cats. Then a prince who was good, handsome and wise began to visit regularly and the princess fell in love with him. But he never mentioned marriage.

So one day she confessed her love for him, and he, in delighted surprise, expressed his for her.

The cats immediately turned to play with the gold balls for the first time in their lives. But it was the prince who became ill, not the princess. The doctors could do nothing and he seemed doomed to die. Despairingly, the princess sought out the sorceress who had made the prediction. The only way to save the prince, she was told, was to spin 10,000 skeins of pure white linen in the twenty-seven days left till Christmas. No hand but hers must spin the skeins and the prince would die at midnight on Christmas night if they were not finished. Rushing home the princess began frantically to spin but by dawn she had accomplished very little. The cats came to see what the trouble was. 'We know what is needed and we can help you,' they said. 'We have paws not hands so we can do the spinning for you, but even for us the time is very short. . . .'

Each cat sat at a spinning wheel and at the end of the day the cats lay asleep by 300 beautiful white skeins of thread. As the days passed and the number of skeins grew the prince's health began to improve. On Christmas day 10,000 skeins were ready for the sorceress and the prince was well. To show her gratitude to the cats she decked them in jewels and they sat upon cushions at the wedding feast. As the festivities wore on the cats curled up on their cushions and suddenly from each was heard a sound like the hum of a spinning wheel. It was the wonderful sound of purring which the cats told the princess was the reward they had received for their help.

In this story the cats' choice of playthings determines whether the princess grows up unharmed by the sorceress, and also the health of the prince. Since the prince represents the sun and the princess is the dawn this means that when the prince is ill it is night-time and until the princess has grown up unharmed by the sorceress of the moonless night and is ready to marry her prince, the dawn cannot come. The time allocated for spinning the wool is twenty-seven days, the time between two full moons; and it is the efforts of the cats that enables the princess to accomplish the apparently impossible task which restores the prince to health. The cats' purring is compared to the noise of the spinning wheel. In Scotland a cat's purr said 'threads and thread ends'. The idea of the sun being trapped by a net of threads was widespread and spinning was thought in some way to affect the passing of the night. In the Irish tale the old woman who sat late to spin was warned by cats to go to bed and was left a silver coin, symbolic of the moon, in the ashes of the fire.

Quite a different sort of story is 'Spiegel the Cat' and yet it too is a moon-myth. Based on a Swiss fairy tale it is a nineteenth-century reworking of traditional material. It recounts the adventures of a cat called Spiegel who lived with a quiet elderly spinster. When she dies the cat has to fend for himself but he is found by the 'Municipal Sorcerer' who takes him home to fatten so that he can use his fat for magical purposes. After trying various subterfuges to stay thin, the cat finally tricks the sorcerer with a fine long tale of his deceased mistress's unhappy love-life and gold coins at the bottom of her well.

The spinster, Spiegel says, once tricked one of her suitors into giving her gold by telling him an untrue story about the poverty of her real lover. Then, when the wedding feast was prepared, the news had come that her lover was dead. Vowing to live as a poor spinster she threw the gold coins down the well. On her death-bed she told Spiegel that if he could find an honest man to wed a poor girl they could have the money and the evil spell on her life would be broken.

The sorcerer, of course, immediately plans to get the gold and the cat promises to help him find a poor girl to marry. Spiegel has a friend, an owl, who lives in the chimney of the house of a witch. This witch is both a church-going old harridan and, when she goes to the Sabbat, a beautiful girl. The owl and the cat catch her in a magic net and threaten to denounce her as a witch unless she marries the sorcerer.

Next day, as a beautiful girl, she waits while Spiegel brings the sorcerer to propose. Unknown to the sorcerer Spiegel and the witch have already been to the well and retrieved the coins. The sorcerer and the witch are married but when the cat and the owl take their leave after the wedding breakfast, she reverts to her old ugly self and the sorcerer realizes that he has been tricked. From then on he must work his spells for her.

The gold coins are sun symbols. The name Spiegel means 'mirror' which is also a symbol of the moon. The owl is a night animal who, with the cat, traps the witch—who is both a beautiful girl and an ugly hag and so represents the phases of the moon—in a magic net or 'cat's cradle' such as was often used for catching and controlling the sun. The spinster, like the witch, is a symbol of the moon. But while the witch is happy to help in the cat's plans as a priestess who carries out a ritual, the spinster is an obscure goddess who must be appeased by the enactment of a dramatic ritual. Her story of deceit was invented by Spiegel. The gold coins had really been stolen by a kinsman and she had thrown them down the well considering them cursed. She was in fact the virgin guardian of the coins like Vesta guarding the eternal fire. In other words, although the moon may appear deceptive as portrayed by the cat and his false story, one cannot take possession of the gold coins, which means obtaining control over the sun, except with the blessing of the Moon-Goddess.

12

For children only

The rose is red, the grass is green,
Serve Queen Bess our noble queen;
   Kitty the spinner
   Will sit down to dinner,
And eat the leg of a frog;
   All good people
   Look over the steeple,
And see the cat play with the dog.
                (*Traditional*)

When printing became common large numbers of penny books or cheap books known as 'chapbooks' were published. These created a demand for many more stories to satisfy a newly literate public. New stories were invented to supplement the traditional ones, muddled versions of old tales appeared and some tales whose underlying meaning was no longer clear were altered to make them interesting to people with a new outlook. In this way stories like 'Puss in Boots' were created and many folk-tales, by being altered for a reading public, lost their mythic impact.

Such is the economy of expression in oral transmission that a seemingly slight variation introduced when a rhyme is committed to the printed page may have a large effect in changing its meaning. When we compare the three versions of this jingle the variations seem very slight indeed:

Great A, little a,
   Bouncing B!
The cat's in the cupboard,
   And she can't see.

A, B, C, tumble down D,
The cat's in the cupboard and can't see me.

For children only

Great A, little a,
Bouncing B!
The cat's in the cupboard,
And she can't see me.

The difference between 'And she can't see' and 'And she can't see me' is hardly noticeable, amounting to the addition of only one word. Yet the first earlier example still has about it a vague idea that something was implied besides the ordinary cat prone to get into cupboards. Surely a cat in a cupboard that 'can't see' is the hidden cat-moon of the moonless night, as black as the inside of a cupboard. The addition of the word 'me' makes it personal and has the effect of changing what had been enigmatic into a simple verse for a child to learn the ABC or bounce a ball by.

Children, who nowadays often know more about such matters than adults, have preserved the idea expressed in the older version in their game of 'Cat's in the Cupboard'. The game consists of one child standing with its back to the rest, at a little distance, or on the other side of the street. The rest of the children gradually advance, chanting the rhyme. Suddenly the 'cat' turns around and tries to catch one of those creeping up. This is the cat-moon behaving treacherously again. In some parts of England hide-and-seek played in the dark is called 'Cat's Eyes' which expresses the same idea of the all-seeing cat in the night.

By inventions, adaptations and alterations traditional material which had been of deep but probably unconscious interest to adult unlettered peasants was converted to become the property of children who could read or be read to. It is now to be found in collections of nursery rhymes and fairy tales. Most nursery rhymes are merely pleasing, but among them are to be found others which accidentally preserve old lore, like a fly in amber.

The rhyme at the beginning of this chapter sounds quite non-sensical but we notice the phrase, 'Kitty the spinner' and recall those other rhymes and stories where cats are concerned with threads and spinning or where a cat offers to bite off the 'threads' of the mice. But who was 'Kitty the spinner'? Did she preside over a now long-forgotten pagan cult to ensure the rebirth of each new day? Was the rhyme originally composed to deliberately hide an apparent nonsense, the hope of the cult's adherents that one day their beliefs would be acceptable to the establishment? Is it a plea to 'All good people [who] look over the steeple' for tolerance? To 'sit down to dinner' together is still very much a mark of acceptance in our own society but an explanation of this rhyme will probably not now be found.

The following cluster of nursery rhymes are about cats taking part in celebrations and weddings where there is music and jollity:

> *The cat sat asleep by the side of the fire,*
> *The mistress snored loud as a pig:*
> *Jack took up his fiddle, by Jenny's desire,*
> *And struck up a bit of a jig.*

> *Hey! diddle diddle,*
> *The cat and the fiddle,*
> *The cow jumped over the moon;*
> *The little dog laugh'd*
> *To see the sport,*
> *And the dish ran after the spoon.*

> *Pussicat, wussicat, with a white foot,*
> *When is your wedding? for I'll come to't.*
> *The beers to brew, the breads to bake,*
> *Pussy-cat, pussy-cat, don't be too late.*

> *A cat came fiddling out of a barn,*
> *With a pair of bagpipes under her arm;*
> *She could sing nothing but fiddle cum fee,*
> *The mouse has married the humble-bee.*
> *Pipe, cat,—dance mouse,*
> *We'll have a wedding at our good house.*

> *Come dance a jig*
> *To my granny's pig,*
> *With a raudy, rowdy, dowdy;*
> *Come dance a jig*
> *To my granny's pig,*
> *And pussy cat shall crowdy.* *

(*A crowdy was an early form of fiddle.)

Cats, mice, pigs, fiddles and bagpipes. We already know that the Celtic corn-goddess could appear in the form of a pig or a cat and the ancients also considered the pig sacred to the moon because, like the cat, its colour ranges from white through red to black; it is prolific but often eats its young (as the shadow of the moon seems to eat its illuminated part), and its tusks are crescent-shaped. Mice symbolized the shadows of the night and the music for the Sabbat was most often supplied by the fiddle and the bagpipes. What is the meaning of a cat's wedding, or a wedding of a mouse and a humble bee with music provided by a cat? The pig belongs to granny, and a cow jumps over the moon. Why does Jenny ask for some fiddling while the cat sleeps by the fire and the mistress snores 'loud as a pig'?

The mouse, as one of the 'grey mice of the shadowy night' marries the bee, that gatherer of golden honey in the sunny day-light hours, who is the day or the sun itself. Here again is the mythical marriage of the sun and the moon which was a theme of folk-tales in all parts of Europe. Granny, as an older woman, was a repository of traditional knowledge and a cow is the female animal *par excellence*. Surely, without labouring the point unduly, all this jollity by female participants in conjunction with symbols of the day and night-time, points to the survival, perhaps quite unconsciously, of a matriarchal cult of the moon and her symbolic marriage with the sun, and celebrations at a witches' Sabbat. Similarly one wonders whether those medieval church carvings which showed cats playing music in the company of pigs and goats may not also have been veiled allusions to then still remembered pagan cults.

What are we to make of the long nursery rhyme 'The Old Woman and the Pig'? It begins as follows:

An old woman was sweeping her house, and she found a little crooked sixpence. What, said she, shall I do with this crooked sixpence? I will go to market and buy a little pig.

As she was coming home, she came to a stile; but the pig would not go over the stile.

She went a little farther, and she met a dog. So she said to the dog—

> *Dog, dog, bite pig!*
> *Pig won't get over the stile,*
> *And I shan't get home to-night.*
> But the dog would not.
>
> *She went a little farther, and she met a stick. So she said—*
> *Stick, stick, beat dog!*
> *Dog won't bite pig;*
> *Pig won't get over the stile,*
> *And I shan't get home to-night.*
> But the stick would not.

—and so on through a long series of a fire being asked to burn the stick, water being asked to quench the fire, an ox to drink the water, a butcher to kill the ox, a rope to hang the butcher, a rat to gnaw the rope and finally a cat to kill the rat. The cat agrees to help the old woman in return for a saucer of milk:

> *So the old woman gave the cat the milk, and when she had lapped up the milk—*
> *The cat began to kill the rat,*
> *The rat began to gnaw the rope,*
> *The rope began to hang the butcher,*
> *The butcher began to kill the ox,*
> *The ox began to drink the water,*
> *The water began to quench the fire,*
> *The fire began to burn the stick,*
> *The stick began to beat the dog,*
> *The dog began to bite the pig,*
> *The pig jumped over the stile,*
> *And so the old woman got home that night.*

The old woman is engaged in sweeping out her house, which is to say she is removing the darkness. Therefore she is a priestess who superintends the transit of the moon which must precede the arrival of the day. A silver sixpence and a pig are clearly moon symbols. So the story is really about the difficulties and dangers which hinder the moon's passage across the night-sky. Not until the cat, a moon-animal who understands the problem and knows what is required, agrees to help is the whole process set in motion and the old woman and her pig get 'home that night'. Day successfully follows night.

This long nursery rhyme is extraordinarily similar to an ancient Hebrew hymn said to have been written originally in the Chaldean language of Babylon. The hymn has been compared to the 'House that Jack Built' nursery rhyme but the resemblance is only superficial as will be seen from the text:

> *A kid, a kid, my father bought*
> *For two pieces of money: A kid, a kid.*
>
> *Then came the cat, and ate the kid,*
> *That my father bought*
> *For two pieces of money: A kid, a kid.*
>
> *Then came the dog, and bit the cat,*
> *That ate the kid*
> *That my father bought*
> *For two pieces of money: A kid, a kid.*
>
> *Then came the staff, and beat the dog,*
> *That bit the cat,*
> *That ate the kid,*
> *That my father bought*
> *For two pieces of money: A kid, a kid.*
>
> *Then came the fire, and burned the staff,*
> *That beat the dog,*
> *etc.—*
>
> *Then came the water, and quenched the fire,*
> *That burned the staff,*
> *etc.—*
>
> *Then came the ox, and drank the water,*
> *That quenched the fire,*
> *etc.—*
>
> *Then came the butcher, and slew the ox,*
> *That drank the water,*
> *etc.—*

Then came the angel of death, and killed the butcher,
That slew the ox,
etc.—

Then came the Holy One, blessed be He!
And killed the angel of death,
etc.—

According to an eighteenth-century interpretation the kid, as a pure animal, represents the Hebrews. The father who purchases it is, of course, Jehovah. The two pieces of money are Aaron and Moses. The Assyrians are symbolized by the cat because they carried the Ten Tribes into captivity. The dog represents the Babylonians and the staff the Persians. Fire indicates the Greek empire. The Romans are symbolized by water and the Saracens by the ox. The butcher who kills the ox is the Crusaders. The Turks are the 'angel of death' who God would destroy when the Jews were restored to their own land under the long-awaited Messiah.

However, if the participants in the Hebrew hymn and those in the rhyme of 'The Old Woman and the Pig' are placed in two columns in the order in which they occur, it will be seen that they correspond, and that the places where they differ are of great interest indeed.

Hebrew Hymn	Old Woman and the Pig
kid	pig
cat	dog
dog	stick
staff	fire
fire	water
water	ox
ox	butcher
butcher	rope
angel of death	rat
Holy One	cat

Kid replaces pig on the Hebrew list and of course the pig, although widely regarded as a symbol of the moon, is an unclean animal for the Jews. For an animal to be pronounced unclean in a religious system means that a long way back in time, in the early and now forgotten evolution of that religion, the animal must have been considered holy. First reserved for ritual meals only, its use as a food would later have become completely taboo. Finally, when the reason for its being taboo was forgotten the animal would be regarded as unclean.

In the Hebrew hymn the cat occurs near the beginning as the treacherous animal which results in the Jews being brought into slavery. But it should be noted that in the whole series it is the one animal who, in the context of the story, is acting out of character. Cats do not eat young goats. It may be objected that wild cats do but this account envisages a farming community and domestic animals. Therefore this cat must either be a late insertion or an introduction from another parallel tradition. If the cat is removed from its position on the Hebrew list and all the others are moved one up, the two lists correspond until almost the bottom.

The 'rope' now comes opposite the 'angel of death'. These seem quite dissimilar but they are both in fact aspects of the same idea on different planes. Both are instruments of death. On the other hand 'rat' and 'Holy One' cannot possibly be equated. However, it may be justifiable to assume that the rat is also a late addition to the story because obviously at the practical level the cat's role was to kill rats. Or, more subtly, the rat may have been inserted for the purpose of hiding the cat's symbolic meaning by stressing its practical function. If the 'rat' in 'The Old Woman and the Pig' can be regarded as a late addition we are left with the next down on the list which is 'cat'. 'Holy One' and 'cat' can be readily equated on the basis that the cat stands for the matriarchal moon-goddess while the Hebrew version speaks of 'God the Father' of the Jewish patriarchs. Thus in one account the old woman bought a pig, and in the other the father bought a kid. If this Jewish version of the tale is really authentic it is further evidence of a matriarchal system having preceded the patriarchal one in Jewish history. The eighteenth-century explanation of this so-called Jewish 'House that Jack Built' now looks much too contrived to be anything other than an intellectual attempt to explain the mysterious list away by arbitrary reference to the history of the Jews in Egypt.

> *There was a crooked man, and he went a crooked mile,*
> *He found a crooked sixpence against a crooked stile:*
> *He bought a crooked cat, which caught a crooked mouse,*
> *And they all lived together in a little crooked house.*

These four terse lines give the briefest possible account of the workings of the solar system and man's age-old preoccupation with magical attempts to ensure that day will follow night. When we compare this nursery rhyme with the 'Old Woman and the Pig' we find that the stile forms a stumbling-block in both. It is the barrier between night and day. In both rhymes a sixpence or moon symbol is found. It is found lodged against the stile by the man after he has 'gone a crooked mile' which is to say the sun has made its way some distance before encountering the obstacle of the stile. The old woman finds her sixpence while cleaning her house which, we saw, meant while she was trying to remove the darkness. In her story it is the pig, another moon symbol, which gets stuck at the stile. When the man finds his moon-helper in the form of a sixpence he buys a cat. His cat-moon then kills the grey mice-shadows of the night. Thus in terms of the domestic regularity implied by the statement that 'they all lived together in a little crooked house' a cosmic regularity is established. A smooth well-run universe in which man can live secure is guaranteed. The fact that everything in the poem is crooked—sixpence, stile, cat, mouse, house, man and mile—was probably originally introduced as a means of protecting secret lore when pagan beliefs were meeting with increasing persecution. It indicates to those in the know, that a cryptic allusion is being made, in the same way as the mention of left-handed or anti-clockwise immediately alerts anyone versed in cabalism to expect something unusual or of special significance.

In the two versions, one Scottish and the other English, of the following familiar nursery rhyme the process by which mythic content is lost has gone much further:

For children only

Pussy cat, pussy cat, where have you been?
I've been up to London to see the queen.
Pussy cat, pussy cat, what did you there?
I frightened a little mouse under her chair.

Poussie, poussie, baudrons,
Where hae ye been?
I've been to London
Seein' the Queen.

Poussie, poussie, baudrons,
What got ye there?
I got a guid fat mousikie
Rinnin' up a stair.

Poussie, poussie, baudrons,
What did ye do wi' t?
I put it in my meal-pock
To eat it to my bread.

To modern readers these are apparently ordinary enough verses about a cat catching a mouse. But why did the action take place in London under the Queen's throne? If this rhyme is looked at alongside the story of the old woman who used her crooked sixpence to buy a pig and whom the cat helped home, and the old man who bought a cat which caught a mouse, it is seen that all three have the same underlying theme. The mouse in the Queen's house is a night-shadow menacing 'the queen of light', the moon. By catching the mouse the cat rescues the moon, with whom she is identified symbolically, from the danger of the shadowy grey mice of the night. Therefore the Scottish rhyme where the mouse is to form part of the cat's lunch is the more recent, although seeming older to English ears because written in dialect Scots. It was secularized and altered by people who could only see the practical matter of a meal at the end as justification for a cat catching a mouse.

These examples of a moon-myth are preserved but not readily understood in children's nursery rhymes. Anyone who has read aloud to children knows that there are hundreds of charming little rhymes and stories about cats and kittens which are totally unrelated to moon-mythology. It is only an occasional reference to old traditions which has managed to slip through the sieve of time and the printing press to survive through a period of general indifference to the present day.

13

Eclipse and reappearance

A house without a cat, and a well-fed well-petted,
and properly revered cat, may be a perfect house,
perhaps, but how can it prove its title?!

(MARK TWAIN)

Early in the sixteenth century, when the church reformer Desiderius Erasmus visited England from Holland he complained in a letter to a friend that a visit to an English home not only involved kissing the host and hostess and their children but also the family cat. From this time the cat gradually increased in popularity as a domestic pet. But during the seventeenth and eighteenth centuries enlightened rationalists, in response to changing social circumstances, altered their attitudes to the traditions of the past. Believing that their destiny was in their own hands they regarded the beliefs and customs, with some of which the cat had in the past been associated, with a mixture of amusement and abhorrence. When beliefs are no longer strongly held they degenerate into superstitions and then become the subjects of satire and sentimentality and so it was with the beliefs for which the cat was a symbol.

Two examples illustrate this process. Frances Teresa Steward, Duchess of Richmond and Lennox, bequeathed annuities to some poor women to enable them to care for her cats after she died. This provoked the poet and critic Alexander Pope to write 'Die, and endow a college or a cat'. Another English aristocrat, Lady Strathmore, even affected a frivolous interest in witchcraft. She once left a dinner party before the dessert had been served, saying that she had to attend the christening of some kittens. The

Scottish witches, of course, had christened the cat which was thrown into the sea to raise a storm and they frequently christened their cat-familiars. So we come full cycle, from religious beliefs, to superstition, to a society fad.

In keeping with the times, writers also lost interest in the symbolic possibilities of the cat. The work of La Fontaine demonstrates this transition. Writing in the seventeenth century he is often described as the last of the fabulists. His early work, for which he drew much of his material from Aesop, has strong mythic undertones but later his writing became more inventive and lost its links with traditional material. In 'The Cockerel, the Cat and the Young Mouse' the symbolic presentation described in Chapter 11 is clearly discernible. The safe daylight hours are represented by the cock while the cat is the pleasant-seeming but treacherous night:

> *A youthful mouse not up to trap,*
> *Had almost met a sad mishap.*
> *The story hear him thus relate,*
> *With great importance, to his mother:—*
> *I passed the mountain bounds of this estate,*
> *And off was trotting on another,*
> *Like some young rat with naught to do*
> *But see things wonderful and new,*
> *When two strange creatures came in view,*
> *The one was mild, benign and gracious;*
> *The other turbulent, rapacious,*
> *With voice terrific, shrill and rough,*
> *And on his head a bit of stuff*
> *That looked like raw and bloody meat,*
> *Raised up a sort of arms, and beat*
> *The Air, as if he meant to fly,*
> *And bore his plumy tail on high.*
> *A cock, that just began to crow,*
> *As if some nondescript,*
> *From far New Holland shipped,*
> *Was what our mousling pictured so.*

He beat his arms, said he, and raised his voice,
And made so terrible a noise,
That I, who, thanks to Heaven, may justly boast
My self as bold as any mouse,
Scud off (his voice would even scare a ghost!)
And cursed himself and all his house;
For, but for him, I should have stayed,
And doubtless an acquaintance made
With her who seemed so mild and good,
Like us, in velvet cloak and hood,
She wears a tail that's full of grace,
A very sweet and humble face,—
No mouse more kindness could desire,—
I do believe that lovely creature
A friend of rats and mice by nature.
Her ears, though, like herself, they're bigger,
Are just like ours in form and figure.
To her I was approaching, when,
Aloft on what appeared his den,
The other screamed,—and off I fled.
My son, his cautious mother said,
That sweet one was the cat,
The mortal foe of mouse and rat,
Who seeks by smooth deceit,
Her appetite to treat.
So far the other is from that,
We yet may eat
His dainty meat;
Whereas the cruel cat,
Whene'er she can, devours
No other meat than ours.

Remember while you live
It is by looks that men deceive.

In 'The Cat and the Two Sparrows', a later poem by La Fontaine, a cat and a sparrow are friends and live together. Then another sparrow flies in and quarrels with the cat's friend. The cat takes his friend's part in the argument and eats the visiting sparrow. Thus he learns that sparrow tastes good and eats his friend too:

> *Now, truly, saith Sir Cat,*
> *I know how sparrows taste by that.*
> *Exquisite, tender, delicate!*
> *This thought soon sealed the other's fate*
> *But hence what moral can I bring?*
> *For, lacking that important thing,*
> *A fable lacks its finishing.*

How right he is: this is a witty tale but it is not a fable and it owed nothing to tradition.

By the early eighteenth century when John Gay wrote about the cats owned by an old woman accused of being a witch (p. 78), he was pouring scorn on beliefs which no longer held any force. Of eighteenth-century poets only Christopher Smart recognized the symbolic possibilities of the cat and he can hardly be considered as a representative of his age. Alcoholism and religious mania forced him from the age of thirty-four to spend seven years of his life in asylums for the insane. While incarcerated he experimented with a form of writing designed for two readers and wrote sets of lines to be declaimed alternately in a statement and response pattern. The well-known 'My Cat Jeoffrey' is not really a poem but a set of lines to be spoken in response to another set which has unfortunately been lost. We can now only conjecture as to what these might have been, and it is impossible to be quite sure that these personal responses would have sounded the same if the more formal statements that they were designed to answer were not missing. The following few lines at least seem to suggest that Christopher Smart was groping towards a restatement of mythic ideas.

> *For when his day's work is done his business more properly begins.*
> *For he keeps the Lord's watch in the night against the adversary.*
> *For he counteracts the powers of darkness by his electrical skin and*
> *glaring eyes.*

For he counteracts the Devil, who is death, by brisking about the life.

For in his morning orisons he loves the sun and the sun loves him.

For he is of the tribe of Tiger.

For the Cherub Cat is a term of the Angel Tiger.

For he has the subtlety and hissing of a serpent, which in goodness he suppresses. . . .

For the Lord commanded Moses concerning the cats at the departure of the Children of Israel from Egypt. . . .

For he made a great figure in Egypt for his signal services.

For he killed the Icneumon-rat very pernicious by land.

Quite what God commanded Moses concerning the cats nobody knows since there is no mention of them in the Bible account of the Jews' exit from Egypt. The ichneumon, of course, is a rat and snake catcher so perhaps Smart confused it with the snake.

Except in the writing of Christopher Smart and the mythical indications which went unnoticed in fairy-tale and nursery rhyme, the old traditions were only able to survive in out-of-the-way parts of the countryside. Perhaps the future will show that the eighteenth and nineteenth centuries were the nadir, or zenith, according to one's point of view, of European man's dissociation from any feeling of mystical identity with the world in which he lived. Sophisticated writers, on the occasions when they took the cat as their subject, treated it with smug condescension. For them the two words which best characterized it were 'cosy' and 'amusing'.

'A kitten,' said Robert Southey, 'is in the animal world what a rosebud is in a garden.' He also invented ridiculous names for his pets. One was called:

The Most Noble the Archduke Rumpelstilzchen, Marquis Macbum, Earle Tomemange, Baron Raticide, Waowler, and Skaratchi.

Typical of the spirit of the age is this facetious poem by Richard Garnett called 'Marigold'.

Eclipse and reappearance

She moved through the garden in glory, because
She had very long claws at the end of her paws.
Her back was arched, her tail was high,
A green fire glared in her vivid eye;
And all the Toms, though never so bold,
Quailed at the martial Marigold.

Neither would it have occurred to Carr-Bosanquet to be anything
other than facetious in his treatment of the events in 'The Dean's
Story', a long poem about the fate of a student who, returning late
to college one night, kicked the college cat. In the middle of the
night the porter was awakened . . .

It was no common cabby
That pealed the midnight bell,
It was a grizzled tabby,
A cat he knew right well;
And lo! behind her through the night
A long procession loomed in sight,
Cats black and yellow, dun and white,
Blue-grey and tortoise-shell.

Their pace was soft and solemn,
Their claws were bared to wound,
In dim fantastic column
A dreadful dirge they crooned.
He counted near three hundred pass
In single file across the grass,
He heard the crash of breaking glass,
That heard, and hearing swooned.

. . .

A help about the dawning
Unlocked the outer door;
She found the window yawning
And snow across the floor,
An empty bed, no blood, no tracks;
No corpse in Cam or on the Backs;
For whom the wrath of Pasht attacks
Is seen on earth no more.

The only clue that fact supplied
I personally verified—
The cats in all the countryside
Were sleeker than before.

Heinrich Heine wrote 'The Witch', a poem about a woman who turns into a cat, but it contains no mystery or horror in the face of incomprehensible forces and it is not to be thought for a moment that Heine believed in it. He was just having some fun at the expense of the superstitious for whom a woman in the form of a cat is no more than a domestic annoyance:

'Dear friends next door, forgive me this intrusion!
I warn you that a witch can cause confusion
By magically altering her form
Into a beast, to do us men much harm.

Your cat's my wife! Indeed, I am awake!
I'm absolutely sure! I can't mistake
Her scent, her sidelong look, her claws,
Her noisy purr, the way she licks her paws.'

The neighbour and his wife cried out in fear—
'Take back the hussy, we don't want her here!'
Their watch-dog barked and made a frightful row,
But puss, quite unperturbed, said gently 'Miaow!'

He did, however, record a boyhood memory of a cat which shows that as a child he could see the poetic possibility that a cat in a dirty attic might be a princess living in an isolated enchanted castle as in fairy tales of old:

. . . It was not exactly an attractive abode, the only creature living there being a fat Angora cat that was not especially given to cleanliness, and that only rarely, with her tail, wiped the dust and the cobwebs partially away from the old rubbish that was stored there.

But my heart was still in the bloom of youth, and the sun shone so merrily through the little dormer window, that everything appeared to me in a fantastic light, and the old cat herself seemed to me like a bewitched princess, who might perhaps suddenly be set free from her animal shape, and show herself in her former beauty and splendour, while at the same time the garret might be changed into a magnificent palace, just as it happens in all fairy-tales.

But this is all forgotten in the witty sonnets he wrote about cats when he was adult.

A Victorian poem for children called 'Mother Tabbyskins' by Elizabeth Anna Hart is an example of how moralizing sentimentality precluded any understanding of mythic content. In another time and setting this poem would have been the story of 'Butter Ears' or 'The Penitent Cat'. It describes how Mother Tabbyskins, a wily old cat, is teaching kittens how to spit and scold when she becomes ill and goes off to bed:

> *Doctor Mouse came creeping,*
> *Creeping to her bed;*
> *Lanced her gums and felt her pulse,*
> *Whispered she was dead.*
> *Very sly, very sly,*
> *The* real *old cat*
> *Open kept her weather eye—*
> *Mouse! beware of that!*
>
> *Old Mother Tabbyskins,*
> *Saying 'Serves him right',*
> *Gobbled up the doctor, with*
> *Infinite delight.*
> *Very fast, very fast,*
> *Very pleasant, too—*
> *'What a pity it can't last!*
> *Bring another, do!'*

Then 'Doctor Dog' comes, the tables are reversed, and Mother Tabbyskins is eaten. The poem ends with a typical Victorian moral:

> *Those who lead the young astray*
> Always *suffer thus.*

It is possible that the last of the great Victorian writers, Thomas Hardy, was a little more aware than most of his contemporaries, of the cat's ability to impress us with its strangeness, to be a symbol of something 'other' even when to the imperceptive it is being quite domestic. At least the fourth verse of his poem 'Last Words to a Dumb Friend' seems to suggest that he was:

> *Strange it is this speechless thing,*
> *Subject to our mastering,*
> *Subject for his life and food*
> *To our gift, and time, and mood;*
> *Timid pensioner of us Powers,*
> *His existence ruled by ours,*
> *Should—by crossing at a breath*
> *Into safe and shielded death,*
> *By the merely taking hence*
> *Of his insignificance—*
> *Loom as largened to the sense*
> *Shape as part, above man's will,*
> *Of the Imperturbable.*

Although not specifically mentioning cats, Mrs. Gaskell, in discussing the difference in temperament between Charlotte and Emily Brontë, has put her finger perhaps on what made the difference between a smug Victorian attitude to cats and an awareness of them as being something apart from, and more than one would expect of, an ordinary household pet. In describing the Brontë sisters' feelings for animals she wrote:

The feeling, which in Charlotte partook of something of the nature of an affection, was, with Emily more of a passion. . . . The helplessness of an animal was its passport to Charlotte's heart; the fierce, wild intractability of its nature was what often recommended it to Emily.

The revival of a more discerning attitude to the cat was greatly stimulated by the enthusiasm for ancient Egypt which followed upon archaeological discoveries. That the comfortable fireside cat was perhaps descended from a cat which had been an object of worship in those far-off exotic times held great appeal and writers and poets soon took advantage of the new imaginative possibilities which were revealed. One of the best examples of this new mood is to be found in the poem simply called 'The Cat' by Giles Lytton Strachey. In it there is a feeling of relief, of relaxation and an expansion of awareness, as if an escape from the constrictions of contemporary society had been found:

Dear creature by the fire a-purr,
Strange idol, eminently bland,
Miraculous puss! As o'er your fur
I trail a negligible hand

And gaze into your gazing eyes,
And wonder in a demi-dream
What mystery it is that lies
Behind those slits that glare and gleam,

An exquisite enchantment falls
About the portals of my sense;
Meandering through enormous halls
I breathe luxurious frankincense.

An ampler air, a warmer June
Enfold me, and my wondering eye
Salutes a more imperial moon
Throned in a more resplendent sky

Than ever knew this northern shore.
Oh, strange! For you are with me too,
And I, who am a cat once more,
Follow the woman that was you.

With tail erect and pompous march,
The proudest puss that ever trod,
Through many a grove, 'neath many an arch,
Impenetrable as a god,

Down many an alabaster flight
Of broad and cedar-shaded stairs,
While over us the elaborate night
Mysteriously gleams and glares!

Eclipse and reappearance

In the poem 'To My Cat' by Graham Tomson it is the aloof inscrutability of the cat 'half loving-kindness and half disdain' which give the impression that it mediates another religion. 'Thine is the love of Ra and Rameses' suggests the tone of the 'Lord's Prayer' but at the same time separates it from that and directs our attention away towards another religion:

> *Half loving-kindliness and half disdain,*
> *Thou comest to my call serenely suave,*
> *With humming speech and gracious gesture grave*
> *In salutation courtly and urbane:*
> *Yet must I humble me thy grace to gain*
> *For wiles may win thee, but no arts enslave,*
> *And nowhere gladly thou abidest, save*
> *Where nought disturbs the concord of thy reign,*
> *Sphinx of my quiet hearth, thou deignest to dwell,*
> *Friend of my toil, companion of my ease,*
> *Thine is the love of Ra and Rameses;*
> *That men forget thou dost remember well,*
> *Beholden still in blinking reveries,*
> *With sombre sea-green gaze inscrutable.*

Gradually, as the cat blinked at the fire in many a Victorian drawing-room, a faint echo from the past was beginning to be heard. It was a more langorous note than had been heard for some time and when it was first paid attention to it produced effects which many would have called unfortunate:

And let me touch those curving claws of yellow ivory, and grasp the tail that like a monstrous asp coils round your heavy velvet paws.

When Oscar Wilde wrote these lines the coiled serpent with its potentialities for good and evil was evoked anew. And with Algernon Swinburne's poem 'To a Cat' a more sensual awareness of the cat has come into being:

Eclipse and reappearance

Stately, kindly, lordly friend
                    Condescend
Here to sit by me, and turn
Glorious eyes that smile and burn,
Golden eyes, love's lustrous meed,
On the golden page I read.

All your wondrous wealth of hair
                    Dark and fair
Silken-shaggy, soft and bright
As the clouds and beams of night,
Pays my reverent hand's caress
Back with friendlier gentleness.

Dogs may fawn on all and some
                    As they come;
You, a friend of loftier mind,
Answer friends alone in kind.
Just your foot upon my hand
Softly bids it understand.

But it was Charles Baudelaire, French poet and critic who, better than anyone of his time, saw that the sensuous cat as an enigmatic symbol, both soothing and disturbing, was a subject worthy of poetic inquiry. A difficult man who loved cats exceedingly he was not himself always easy to like. We are indebted to his friend Théophile Gautier, a cat-lover himself, who described cats as 'tigers of poor devils', for his sympathetic account of Baudelaire's obsession with cats.

Baudelaire would coax any cat he saw in the street to come and be stroked but Gautier found his friend's excitability and excessive delight in cats and everything else which caught his fancy, exhausting. He saw clearly that Baudelaire's fascination for the seemingly sinister qualities of the cat's nature corresponded to the poet's character and interests which led him to reject many of the values of contemporary society and to the creation of the 'Fleurs du Mal' poems. 'There is to these pretty creatures . . .' wrote Gautier:

a nocturnal side, mysterious and cabalistic, which had much attraction for the poet. A cat, with its phosphorescent eyes that stand it in the stead of lanterns, and sparks flashing from its back, moves fearlessly through the darkness, where it meets wandering ghosts, witches, alchemists, necromancers, resurrectionists, lovers, thieves, murderers, grey-coated patrols, and all the obscure larvae that emerge and work by night only. It seems to know more than the latest special from the sabbath, and does not hesitate to rub up against Mephistopheles' lame leg. Its serenades under the balconies of the female of its kind, its amours on the roof to the accompaniment of yells like those of a child being murdered, impart to it a passably devilish look that, up to a certain point, justifies the repugnance felt for it by the practical, daylight minds, for whom the mysteries of Erebus have no attraction. But Doctor Faust will always love to have a cat for a companion in his study filled with tomes and alchemic apparatus. Baudelaire himself was a voluptuous, wheedling cat, with velvety manners, mysterious gait, strong and supple, casting on men and things a glance filled with a troublous, free, insistent light, difficult to retain, but wholly free from perfidiousness, and faithfully attached to those to whom he had once given his independent sympathy.

Both men liked to have a cat in their room when they were working. For them its patient silence and seemingly feminine delicacy of movement made it at once companion and muse as Baudelaire acknowledges in these two examples from 'Fleurs du Mal'.

I

A Cat is walking in my brain
As in his room—a gentle, strong
And charming cat whose miauling song
Is so discreet as to remain

Well-nigh inaudible; but calm
Or querulous, no matter which,
His voice is always deep and rich.
There is his secret and his charm.

Eclipse and reappearance

In strains that ripple and that filter
Throughout my darkest being, he
Enchants me as with poetry,
Or with the magic of some philtre.

His voice can lull the cruellest ill;
All ecstasies are in its range;
Long though the phrases be, his strange
Song without words can work its spell.

No, there is no bow than can sing
Upon that instrument, my heart,
And make such royal music start
From its most thrilling, vibrant string

As thou, cat, with thy witchery,
Seraphic creature, mystical,
In whom, as in an angel, all
Is harmony and subtlety.

II

The magic perfume of the cat
Is such that, having stroked the fur
Of mine but once, I was aware
That I too was perfumed by it.

The genius of the place is he,
Inspirer, judge of his domain,
Where no one may dispute his reign.
Is he some sprite or deity?

When from my dear cat's eyes that claim
Me like a magnet mine return,
And with docility in turn
They peer into my soul again,

To my astonishment I see
Pale pupils pouring out their rays;
Bright beacons, living opals, gaze
And contemplate me fixedly.

Ripe lovers and philosophers both love
The strong and gentle cat, pride of the home,
For he, like them, is wont to keep his room,
And, sensitive to cold, is loath to move.

A devotee of thought and ecstasy,
He seeks the haunts of silence, dark and lonely,
Fit steed of gloom for Erebus, if only
He could have bent his pride to slavery!

Stretched pensively in noble attitudes,
Like sphinxes dreaming in their solitudes,
He seems to ponder in an endless trance;

With magic sparks his fecund loins are filled,
And, like fine sand, bright golden atoms gild
With vague and starry rays his mystic glance.

Another friend of Baudelaire and Gautier was the painter Manet. He too was fond of cats and designed a poster to advertise Gautier's book *Les Chats*. Indeed it has been suggested that the title of Manet's famous painting *Olympia* does not refer to the woman in the picture at all but to the black cat at her feet. According to this theory Manet painted the black woman in order to enlarge the black area of the cat set off by the pale nude on the bed. Although in reproductions of the oil painting of *Olympia* the cat does not show up particularly clearly, in a water colour and an engraving of the same subject by Manet the cat with a lithe twisting tail above its head is clearly part of the composition, acting as a balance for the erect tense pose of the woman's head with a black ribbon bow at the neck. Baudelaire actually wrote to Manet asking 'is it really the cat?' Unfortunately Manet's reply is not known.

Whether Manet's *Olympia* is intended to be the black cat or not, a cat could quite explicitly be the lover for Baudelaire:

Come, lovely cat, and rest upon my heart,
And let my gaze dive in the cold
Live pools of thine enchanted eyes that dart
Metallic rays of green and gold.

Eclipse and reappearance

My fascinated hands caress at leisure
Thy head and supple back, and when
Thy soft electric body fills with pleasure
My thrilled and drunken fingers, then

Thou changest to my woman; for her glance,
Like thine, most lovable of creatures,
Is icy, deep, and cleaving as a lance.

And round her hair and sphinx-like features
And round her dusky form float, vaguely blent,
A subtle air and dangerous scent.

Baudelaire in his poetry experimented with the cat's symbolic possibilities: companion of the quiet contemplative, lover, portent of the mysteries of the underworld, meditator on eternity, and inducer of mystic insight. The cat's sensuous allure is disturbingly female. It is bewitching. 'Is he some sprite or deity?' he asks. From what we know of the excesses and contrasts of his life, his attraction to cats, and his poems about them, there begins to emerge a philosophy which is very different from that accepted by the society in which he lived.

In the poem called 'Confession' Baudelaire explores the idea of an unavoidable fate which awaits those who love a mysterious female symbolized by the cat:

Your arm, bewitching woman, once, only once,
Was linked in my arm, smooth and slim,
(Upon my soul's sad background, dark and lonely,
That memory has not grown dim.)

'Twas late; round as a bright new coin the moon
Shone forth, and pale solemnity
Bathed Paris sleeping in the night's high noon
And flooded it with sorcery.

Beneath the carriage gateways, with cocked ear,
The cats were prowling furtively,
Or, shadow-like, companions dark and dear,
They slowly walked with thee and me.

Eclipse and reappearance

When, suddenly, amid this tête-à-tête
    That flowered in the silver night,
From you, rich instrument who but vibrate
    With radiancy and gay delight,

From you, as joyous as a fanfare in
    The sparkling morn, escaped a thin
Strange note, grotesque and sorrowful and wild,
    That staggered like a crippled child,

A sickly, foul and sombre infant whom
    Its shrinking kin would blush to own
And who from men's eyes in a cellar's gloom
    Had been concealed, to pine alone!

Your poor voice shrilly sang 'that here below
    Naught's sure; that though 'tis overlaid
With painted lies, the truth will out, and so
    The self-seeking of man's betrayed;

That being a lovely woman's no light task,
    That 'tis to use the banal wiles
Of frigid dancers swooning 'neath a mask
    Of sham and automatic smiles;

That to build on hearts is folly past belief;
    That love and beauty come to grief,
Until Oblivion throws them in its hod
    To bear them back again to God!'

I've oft evoked that moon's enchanted light,
    That langour, hush, and horrible
Strange confidence once whispered in the night
    Within the heart's confessional.

This bewitching woman with whom he walked 'once only once' in the moonlight, although seemingly gay and loving, bore the insight:

    That to build on hearts is folly past belief;
        That love and beauty come to grief,
    Until Oblivion throws them in its hod
        To bear them back again to God!

They stroll in the moonlight, and most curiously in the third verse we are told that their walk is accompanied by cats:

> *Beneath the carriage gateways, with cocked ear,*
> *The cats were prowling furtively*
> *Or, shadow-like, companions dark and dear,*
> *They slowly walked with thee and me.*

In these two verses he is rejecting a god of loving forgiveness and hinting at a goddess, a compelling and mysterious woman accompanied by cats. She it is who while seeming to be loving knows, because she has seen the other side of the coin of life, that love can be replaced by its opposite and that the only release is in oblivion. It is moonlight and the cats walk with them. This is Isis, the Mother Goddess and Freya: *La Belle Dame Sans Merci!*

After a long lapse of time during which the cat as a symbol had apparently fallen into disuse, Baudelaire turned to it again, stressing the ambivalent, loving and treacherous qualities which the cat by its nature symbolizes. Studies of the Orient, comparative religion and anthropology, and discoveries in archaeology expanded men's horizons and opened a window through which societies organized differently from their own could be glimpsed. Practical rationality began to be seen as a restriction rather than as the liberating tool it had promised to be. It was in such a climate that Baudelaire and others rediscovered the cat.

14

Making believe

It is a very inconvenient habit of kittens
(Alice had once made the remark) that,
whatever you say to them they *always* purr.
(LEWIS CARROLL)

The Anglo-Irish writer W. B. Yeats who was born in 1865 was
fortunate to be able to maintain contact with a corner of Europe
where the older ways of thinking continued to exist. There it was
customary for people, deceptively called simple, to deal with more
than one layer of meaning at the same time. His experience of
Irish ways had a profound effect upon his creative writing and he
also collected many items of folk-lore and story which have
helped piece together traditions which had disappeared elsewhere.
In much of his writing Yeats was concerned to reinstate the
importance of intuition against rationality which had for so long
been the yardstick by which all activities were judged.

In his playlet about a blind beggar and a lame beggar, Yeats
uses the symbolism of the cat to draw attention to the possibility
of there being other levels upon which events may be judged
besides the practical. The play tells of a blind beggar who has
carried a lame beggar on his back to St. Colman who lives beside
a healing well. There the supplicants may either ask the Saint to
heal their infirmity or to bless them. The blind beggar chooses to
regain his sight and the lame beggar decides to remain lame and
to become one of the blessed. St. Colman then mounts upon the
lame beggar's back who henceforth must carry him. The following poem, 'Minnaloushe', Yeats wrote to be sung, one verse at
the beginning, one in the middle and one at the end of the
play:

Making believe

The cat went here and there
And the moon spun round like a top,
And the nearest kin of the moon,
The creeping cat, looked up.
Black Minnaloushe stared at the moon,
For, wander and wail as he would,
The pure cold light in the sky
Troubled his animal blood.

Minnaloushe runs in the grass
Lifting his delicate feet.
Do you dance, Minnaloushe, do you dance?
When two close kindred meet,
What better than call a dance?
Maybe the moon may learn,
Tired if that courtly fashion,
A new dance turn.

Minnaloushe creeps through the grass
From moonlight place to place,
The sacred moon overhead
Has taken a new phase.
Does Minnaloushe know that his pupils
Will pass from change to change,
And that from round to crescent,
From crescent to round they range?
Minnaloushe creeps through the grass
Alone, important and wise,
And lifts to the changing moon
His changing eyes.

But the play itself has nothing whatever to do with cats and
in the notes to it Yeats says:

It has pleased me to think that the half of me that feels can
sometimes forget all that belongs to the more intellectual half
but a few images. The night's dream takes up and plays in the
same forgetful fashion with our waking thoughts. Minnaloushe

and the Moon were perhaps—it all grows faint to me—an exposition of man's relation to what I have called the Antithetical Tincture, and when the Saint mounts upon the back of the Lame Beggar he personifies a certain great spiritual event which may take place when Primary Tincture, as I have called it, supersedes Antithetical—'The burning bow . . . is drawn between deformity of body and mind.'

In language that has already become difficult for us to understand Yeats is saying that the mystery of the cat and the relationship of its mysterious changing eyes to the moon and its changing phases is here intended to draw attention to the fact that things are often other than they seem. A burden is only a burden in a certain context. The beggar who has regained his sight will never see what the lame beggar *sees*. He has been made whole in a much wider sense. Using the logic of dreams, Yeats intends us to understand that the moon and the cat, because of their changefulness, stand for the changes, of quite different orders from each other, that have overtaken the two beggars.

There were two Victorian writers who had already done what Yeats was suggesting. Without really being aware of it they had allowed the half that feels to 'forget all that belongs to the more intellectual half but a few images'. The results were not works of great intensity and insight such as those of Yeats or Baudelaire, but were works of humour. These two were of course, Lewis Carroll and Edward Lear, and unlike Baudelaire and Yeats they seem at the conscious level to have remained unaware that the cats they immortalized had any symbolic meaning.

At the time that Carroll and Lear were writing their charming apparent nonsense the Age of Enlightenment had become singularly unilluminating when applied to such fields as myth, folklore and traditional beliefs. What had started out so full of promise for the emancipation of the mind had become in England the narrow mechanical outlook characteristic of the Victorians. Sir James Frazer's book *The Golden Bough* and the writings of Sigmund Freud which asserted our indissoluble links with the primitive, the intuitive and the unconscious were still in the future and their effects were to percolate slowly. The poet and critic Kathleen Raine tells us that in the 1890s when her father was a student, the poem 'Kubla Khan' was considered '. . . to be a poem of great beauty but utterly meaningless, but at the same time, how Victorians turned to "non-sense" as an escape from their self-inflicted mental limitations, producing in the realm of the "purely fictitious" such masterpieces as Alice in Wonderland, the Nonsense of Edward Lear. . . .' By such means people were beginning, without being aware of what was happening, to find their way back (or down) from the surface of things which for long they had mistakenly thought to be their only aspect. They were beginning to recognize that there were other realities just as real as the outward appearances upon which they had concentrated.

With the benefit of hindsight and the works of Freud and Jung at our elbow it is easy to psycho-analyse the Victorians. For them Lear and Carroll wrote humorous nonsense, and yet on Jungian principles possibly both authors and some at least of their readers, would have been unconsciously aware of a meaning in the apparent absurdities. How soothing to the stern Victorian breast must Edward Lear's 'The Owl and the Pussy Cat' have been:

I

The Owl and the Pussy-Cat went to sea
  In a beautiful pea-green boat,
They took some honey, and plenty of money,
Wrapped up in a five-pound note.
The Owl looked up to the stars above,
  And sang to a small guitar,
'O lovely Pussy! O Pussy, my love,
'What a beautiful Pussy you are,
    'You are,
    'You are!
'What a beautiful Pussy you are!'

II

Pussy said to the Owl, 'You elegant fowl!
'How charmingly sweet you sing!
'O let us be married! too long we have tarried
'But what shall we do for a ring?'
They sailed away for a year and a day,
To the land where the Bong-tree grows,
And there in a wood a Piggy-wig stood,
With a ring at the end of his nose,
His nose,
His nose,
With a ring at the end of his nose.

III

'Dear Pig, are you willing to sell for one shilling
'Your ring?' Said the Piggy, 'I will'.
So they took it away, and were married next day
By the Turkey who lives on the hill.
They dined on mince, and slices of quince,
Which they ate with a runcible spoon;
And hand in hand, on the edge of the sand,
They danced by the light of the moon,
The moon,
The moon,
They danced by the light of the moon.

The owl and the cat, both night animals, sailed away for a year and a day in a sheltering boat on a sea representing the primordial waters from which life was created. The old Moon-Goddess's year was thirteen lunar months making 364 days, plus one day which brought the total to 365. The pig, especially one standing in a wood which symbolizes night, is sacred to the Moon. For one silver shilling, a moon symbol, it sells them a sun symbol—the ring from the end of its nose. That the cat and the owl dance by the light of the moon is to be expected. They then dine upon quince, the first cultivated apple, sacred to Aphrodite, the Goddess of Love. Lear was delighted when his friend Edward Strachey pointed out to him that in dining upon quince his owl and pussy cat were reviving a sixth-century B.C. Greek law whereby the Athenian bride and groom were required to eat a quince together at their wedding. Although Lear seems to have been fascinated by the mere sound of the word 'runcible' (his poems contain a 'runcible cat' and even a 'runcible hat'), a runcible spoon is a three-pronged fork hollowed in the shape of a spoon. This could be interpreted as analogous to the sistrum which for the Egyptians was a fertility symbol. The hollow spoon is obviously a female symbol and the three prongs of the fork may be taken to represent the three aspects, lover, mother and eventual destroyer of the Goddess of Love. In 'The Pobble Who Has No Toes', the sailors, who have a habit of knowing about such things, say that the Pobble has

> . . . *gone to fish, for his Aunt Jobiska's*
> *Runcible Cat with crimson whiskers!*

Only very special cats have crimson whiskers. As it was a 'Runcible Cat' which for Lear would have recalled the runcible spoon and unconsciously suggested the goddess, the 'Runcible Cat with crimson whiskers' must be like the cat Blanchette or the maiden Cat-skin who wore beautiful dresses to represent either the full moon or the resplendent sunrise.

Menacing cats and also quite ordinary cats occur in Lear's writings. Not all of them were loaded with symbolic meaning. When he wrote the limerick about the 'Young Person of Smyrna, Whose grandmother threatened to burn her' Lear could not have read Sir James Frazer's account of the cat's substitution for a human sacrifice because *The Golden Bough* was not published till after Lear died.

In the publisher's preface to the Frederick Warne edition of the *Nonsense Omnibus*, published in 1943, it is said that 'Lear's fantastic absurdities are as void of symbolic meaning as they are of vulgarity and cynicism; they are nonsense pure and simple, and that is their charm'. This may well be true of most of his output, but not surely of 'The Owl and the Pussy Cat'. It is interesting to compare it with another contemporary so-called 'nonsense' poem, the anonymous rhyme 'Dame Wiggins of Lee' published in 1823, when Lear was eleven years old.

Dame Wiggins of Lee was a worthy old soul
As e'er threaded a needle, or washed in a bowl;
She held mice and rats in such antipathy,
That seven fine cats kept Dame Wiggins of Lee.

The rats and mice scared by this fierce-whiskered crew,
The seven poor cats soon had nothing to do;
So, as anyone idle she ne'er wished to see,
She sent them to school, did Dame Wiggins of Lee.

But soon she grew tired of living alone,
So she sent for her cats from school to come home:
Each rowing a wherry, returning, you see—
The frolic made merry Dame Wiggins of Lee.

To give them a treat she ran out for some rice;
When she came back they were skating on ice.
'I shall soon see one down. Aye, perhaps two or three,
I'll bet half-a-crown,' said Dame Wiggins of Lee.

While, to make a nice pudding, she went for a sparrow,
They were wheeling a sick lamb home in a barrow.
'You shall all have some sprats for your humanity,
My seven good cats' said Dame Wiggins of Lee.

While she ran to the field, to look for its dam,
They were warming the bed for the poor sick lamb;
They turned up the clothes as neat as could be:
'I shall ne'er want a nurse,' said Dame Wiggins of Lee.

She wished them good-night, and went up to bed;
When lo! in the morning the cats were all fled.
But soon—what a fuss! 'Where can they all be?
Here, pussy, puss, puss!' cried Dame Wiggins of Lee.

The Dame's heart was nigh broke, so she sat down to weep,
When she saw them come back, each riding a sheep;
She fondled and patted each purring Tommy:
'Ah, welcome, my dears!' said Dame Wiggins of Lee.

The Dame was unable her pleasure to smother,
To see the sick lamb jump up to its mother.
In spite of the gout, and a pain in her knee,
She went dancing about, did Dame Wiggins of Lee.

This is truly 'devoid of symbolic meaning'. If the 'Owl and the Pussy Cat' is nonsense then 'Dame Wiggins of Lee' is not nonsense but rubbish. It illustrates the difference between a poem which while claiming to be nonsense is in touch, even if unconsciously, with an underlying stream of awareness; and one that is a consciously contrived attempt at facetiousness. One captivates us although it is 'nonsense' in the sense of being nonrational; the other never captures our imagination at all because it never makes any contact with the layers of awareness where the source of imaginative creation lies.

Sir Edward Strachey in his introduction to the same edition of the *Nonsense Omnibus* opposes nonsense to common sense which must remain prosaic and commonplace:

> Nonsense has proved not to be an equally prosaic and commonplace negative of Sense, not a mere putting forward of incongruities and absurdities, but the bringing out a new and deeper harmony of life in and through its contradictions. Nonsense in fact, in this use of the word, has shown itself to be a true work of the imagination, a child of genius, and its writing one of the Fine Arts.

Kathleen Raine would agree. For the Victorian it was only possible to approach the mythical through apparent nonsense. As she says in her book *Defending Ancient Springs* '. . . all these are excursions into the mythical made possible on the pretext of make-believe . . .'

Lewis Carroll was contemporary with Edward Lear: famous for his *Alice* books he was not so well known as Charles Lutwidge Dodgson, mathematician and logician. Peter and Iona Opie point out that Carrollian humour 'often arises from Dodgson's application of sound logic to a ridiculous situation: the resulting sense of fitness being one of the reasons his verse and stories are so memorable.' His appreciation of the often ludicrous fitness of appearances to be found in everyday occurrences was his great gift. When seeming to be most mad his stories never cease to be logical, conforming to an inner logic of their own. In *Alice in Wonderland* the self-confessedly mad Cheshire Cat had a logical argument to prove its insanity. As he explained to Alice:

'. . . a dog growls when it's angry, and wags it's tail when it's pleased. Now *I* growl when I'm pleased, and wag my tail when I'm angry. Therefore I'm mad.'

It then withdrew leaving its grin behind! Wonderland, as Alice kept discovering to her cost, was a place where common sense did not operate. They were all mad there and she would not have come unless she was mad too, the Cheshire Cat tells her.

Throughout the whole adventure Alice longed to get back to her own cat, Dinah, whose name is very close to Diana, the Goddess of Hunting who once turned into a cat. To Alice, Dinah is only her loved pet and she does not appreciate that her descriptions of its exploits reveal the other aspect of Diana and are terrifying to the animals that assemble by the pool of tears.

Near the end of *Alice Through the Looking Glass* Alice complains that whatever you say to kittens they only purr. What could be more ordinary than this? Of course kittens only purr. Yet Carroll, by making Alice express dissatisfaction at this state of affairs, prompts us to feel, as Alice does, that cats *ought* somehow to communicate more. Alice is beginning to suspect that there is something odd about cats.

Alice Through the Looking Glass was published six years after *Alice in Wonderland* and in it the symbolic role of the cats is clearer. In both the *Alices* the action takes place in a non-real setting. In the first book this is established as down an impossible rabbit-hole and through a mysterious tiny door: in the second an unreal world is immediately established by crossing to the other side of the mirror where the realities of the normal world are reversed. It will be recalled that in the Swiss tale of 'Spiegel the Cat' the cat's name meant 'mirror' and Robert Graves tells us that in the course of the history of painting, changes in artistic

conventions have resulted in a mirror being placed in the hand of
the Love Goddess where once a quince was shown.

A black kitten and a white kitten, both daughters of Alice's real
cat, Dinah, are in Looking Glass Land the Red and White Queens
of the chess game. The White Queen is benign and the Red Queen
is rather unpleasant. Evidently they represent the helpful full
moon and the treacherous moonless night, or the two aspects of
the life-giving and life-taking Great Mother-Goddess. At the end
of the tale Alice herself becomes a Queen—a priestess to the
Mother-Goddess perhaps? What an unthinkable aspiration for a
nicely brought up little girl in Victorian England! By means of an
apparently nonsensical story Lewis Carroll has found for Alice,
and anyone else who cares to partake of the adventure, a way back
through the looking-glass. And having crossed this mysterious
barrier between what is considered real and the apparently
fantastic, to discover that both have their own logic and internal
consistency. This is the point which Robert Graves makes in his
poem 'Alice':

> *When the prime heroine of our nation, Alice,*
> *Climbing courageously in through the Palace*
> *Of Looking Glass, found it inhabited*
> *By chessboard personages, white and red,*
> *Involved in never-ending tournament,*
> *She being of a speculative bent*
> *Had long foreshadowed something of the kind,*
> *Asking herself: 'Suppose I stood behind*
> *And viewed the fireplace of Their drawing-room*
> *From hearthrug level, why must I assume*
> *That what I'd see would need to correspond,*
> *With what I now see? And the rooms beyond?*

> *Proved right, yet not content with what she had done,*
> *Alice decided to increase her fun:*
> *She set herself, with truly British pride*
> *In being a pawn and playing for her side,*
> *And simple faith in simple strategum,*
> *To learn the rules and moves and perfect them.*

Making believe

So prosperously there she settled down
That six moves only and she'd won her crown—
A triumph surely! But her greater feat
Was rounding these adventures off complete:
Accepting them, when safe returned again,
As queer but true—not only in the main
True, but as true as anything you'd swear to,
The usual three dimensions you are heir to.
For Alice though a child could understand
That neither did this chance-discovered land
Make nohow or contrariwise the clean
Dull round of mid-Victorian routine,
Nor did Victoria's golden rule extend
Beyond the glass: it came to the dead end
Where empty hearses turn about; thereafter
Begins that lubberland of dream and laughter,
The red-and-white-flower-spangled hedge, the grass
Where Apuleius pastured his Gold Ass,
Where young Gargantua made whole holiday . . .
But further from our heroine not to stray,
Let us observe with what uncommon sense—
Though a secure and easy reference
Between Red Queen and Kitten could be found—
She made no false assumption on that ground
(A trap in which the scientist would fall)
That queens and kittens are identical.

No, Victoria's golden rule did not extend beyond the glass. There where the dreary 'empty hearses turn about' a different joyful world began:

> *Where Apuleius pastured his Gold Ass*
> *Where young Gargantua made whole holiday . . .*

Alice saw that both these worlds had validity. One of them did not 'make nohow' of the other. It makes no sense therefore to drag either queens or kittens through the mirror-line of demarcation. Kittens and queens are not the *same*. The kitten on this side of the mirror is the symbol 'queen' on the other. When the blind beggar in Yeats' play regained his sight this could not be compared with what happened to the lame beggar. Their experiences happened on different planes, on different sides of the mirror. Minnaloushe presides as one man's consciousness is raised to a higher level. Alice's kittens dissolve through the looking-glass of our own imagination that walls us into a particular form of reality and frees us to play with all the associations which symbols, including that of the cat, may put in our laps. We too may enjoy 'whole holiday' with Gargantua.

15

For ever and ever

A god among creatures—
Yet also a stray like me.
(TONY ROSS)

The eighteenth and nineteenth centuries, often called the Age of Enlightenment, was a period when a rational approach to life was paramount and the old mythic modes of expression almost died away. But already, before studies in anthropology and psychology had shown how limiting a solely rational approach to life could be the Victorian Era had thrown up two authors whose humorous writing had, as we saw in the last chapter, unconsciously, by-passed the rational. Since then the twentieth century has witnessed the emergence of a greater understanding of the importance of symbolism. Although there is still a great deal of humorous writing about cats this does not carry any hidden mythic meanings within it because the climate of opinion now permits a serious interest in the psychological truths that symbols can convey. Fashions in the means of expressing religious and artistic ideas, and the world we live in, may change beyond recognition yet a basic need remains unchanged. Man must still relate his individual life to existence in an impersonal, uncaring world. In the past the cat has proved to be an indestructible but adaptable symbol. Is it capable of further transformations to suit our life and times?

Examination of the vast amount of twentieth-century writing in which cats occur shows that there are writers who have consciously set out to retell the old mythic tales in modern form and in so doing have kept the old tales alive by making them more interesting to modern readers. Others unconsciously or accident-ally evoke the mythic images without deliberately setting out to

179

do so. Finally there is the possibility that a writer may completely transform the symbolic use of the cat. In this case the changes are seen to be of the same order of magnitude as those which occurred, for instance, when a cat sacred to a mother-goddess was transformed into a Cat-King.

The story called 'The Traveller from the East and the Traveller from the West' by Sylvia Townsend Warner is a deliberate retelling of Aesop's fable called 'Metamorphosis' in which Aphrodite changed a cat into a woman. It is the tale of a forlorn man amongst a group of people at an inn. When a cat under a table catches a mouse he faints. After being revived he tells them his story. He had fallen in love with a very beautiful girl, flaxen-haired and with green eyes. Her grace of movement fascinated him and he had loved to watch her play tennis. They were married and on the wedding night he began to caress his beautiful languorous bride, when . . .

> . . . suddenly, her whole demeanour changed, her face grew sharp, her eyes gleamed with excitement and even squinted, and the hand that had been pinching my ear now swept over my cheek and ripped it open with a finger-nail. She quivered, she drew her limbs together. And in a flash she leaped out of bed and began to spring madly about the room. She was chasing a little mouse.
>
> . . . All the grace, all the lightness and agility I had admired became horrible to me as I watched her prancing about the room, casting herself hither and thither, catching the mouse and letting it go again, catching it again, and tossing it in the air and catching it in her jaws as it fell. At last she settled down in a corner and ate it. And when she had finished this frightful meal she came towards the bed, walking a little unsteadily as though she were drunk, with her eyes serenely clear and her brow as bland and pure as a lily.
>
> 'You must forgive me,' she said. 'My grandfather married a white Angora, and so my blood is one-quarter Cat. All the fur is inside, thank heaven! But when I see a mouse I cannot resist it.'

Here she is, as she was at the beginning of Europe's story-telling, still beautiful but still treacherous, horrifying and unpredictable.

Similarly, 'Frog Chorus' by Douglas Stewart is an example of a poem in which it is very easy to recognize the old conflict produced by the changing nature of the moon. Grandfather Toad is almost caught by the black and silent cat-demon with green moon-eyes but is saved by 'the lady'—that shadowy, moonlit thing who lives with the cat-demon in 'her enormous house' which is, of course, the enchanted castle of fairy tale. Grandfather Toad well knows the two-faced aspect of the goddess who must be sung to 'with groans and bells as long as there are frogs in pools':

> *Grandfather Toad, Grandfather Toad,*
> *The moon shines bright on our damp abode,*
> *The stone is a brother and the log is a friend—*
> *Tell us that story about the fiend.*
>
> *'Black and silent that demon runs*
> *With glaring eyes like two green moons;*
> *And round the devil's mouth, my dears,*
> *Not whiskers grow but blood-stained spears;*
> *And you are looking on one who saw*
> *His lashing tail, his naked claw,*
> *And watched his wet lips bare his teeth,*
> *And smelled his great hot meaty breath.'*
>
> *Grandfather Toad, Grandfather Toad,*
> *Was it long ago, is the devil dead?*
> *Somebody told us the fiend could swim—*
> *Is it safest down at the bottom of the dam?*
>
> *'As I was crossing the moonlit lawn*
> *With a hundred yards to hop by dawn*
> *(Ah, toads could travel when I was young!)*
> *I saw that tomcat crouch and spring.*
> *I hopped, I screamed, yes, screaming and hopping*
> *I fled from the paw that kept just tipping,*
> *For he takes his time in that last hour*
> *When you die in his green eyes' blinding glare.'*

For ever and ever

Grandfather Toad, you are brave and good
But the night seems chill as a black snake's blood.
Thick is the bush and the dead leaves crack—
Tell us about the lady, quick!

'Oh, round that tall and glittering form
Her dark hair blew like clouds of storm,
And shade and moonlight seemed to chase
Like windblown gumleaves round her face;
And out of that great hollow stone
—The house of the fiend—I saw her run;
She scolds that devil, she's stooping, and—
Grandfather Toad in that white hand!'

Her hand was soft and gentle and warm,
She tickled your backbone, she meant no harm;
Grandfather Toad, if she's what you said,
Why wouldn't she strike that devil down dead?

'She is that shadowy, moonlit thing
Whose praise each night you chirrup and sing
While elderly toads must rumble and groan
To make that beauty all their own;
And though in her enormous house
She feeds the devil and lets him loose,
She shall be sung with groans and bells
As long as there are frogs in pools.'

Groan in the shadow, groan on the stones,
Grandfather Toad saw the devil once.
But Grandfather Toad he's a saint and a seer
And we can't help singing while the moon shines clear.

By contrast, we find that unlike the updated version of Aesop's 'Metamorphosis', when Edith Sitwell wrote her poem 'Dark Song' she did not consciously intend to recreate a myth. She was extremely interested in symbolism but in describing the poem she says only that it is about the 'beginnings of things and their relationship':

For ever and ever

The fire was furry as a bear
And the flames purr . . .
The brown bear rambles in his chain
Captive to cruel men
Through the dark and hairy wood . . .
The maid sighed, 'All my blood
Is animal. They thought I sat
Like a household cat;
But through the dark woods rambled I . . .
Oh, if my blood would die!'
The fire had a bear's fur;
It heard and knew . . .
The dark earth, furry as a bear,
Grumbled too!

Yet reading it we can see that the animal nature of the girl whose spirit wanders in the forest and the simile 'like a household cat' evoke the fairy-tale characters Cat-Skin and Blanchette.

A poem by Ted Hughes called 'Esther's Tom Cat' might also be thought to invoke a 'Cat King' in the same way as Edith Sitwell's poem calls Cat-Skin to mind. But although his poem is about a violent untameable animal whose experiences stretch back in time from ashcans through medieval adventures to an identification of its eyes and outcry with the moon, Ted Hughes is more interested in history than myth. 'Esther's Tom Cat' is therefore more likely to be about an actual cat upon whose antecedents we are invited to speculate:

Daylong this tomcat lies stretched flat
As an old rough mat, no mouth and no eyes.
Continual wars and wives are what
Have tattered his ears and battered his head.

Like a bundle of old rope and iron
Sleeps till blue dusk. Then reappear
His eyes, green as ringstones: he yawns wide red,
Fangs fine as a lady's needle and bright.

For ever and ever

A tomcat sprang at a mounted knight,
Locked round his neck like a trap of hooks
While the knight rode fighting its clawing and bite.
After hundreds of years the stain's there

On the stone where he fell, dead of the tom:
That was at Barnborough. The tomcat still
Grallochs odd dogs on the quiet,
Will take the head clean off your simple pullet.

Is unkillable. From the dog's fury,
From gunshot fired point-blank he brings
His skin whole, and whole
From owlish moons of bekittenings.

Among ashcans. He leaps and lightly
Walks upon sleep, his mind on the moon.
Nightly over the round world of men,
Over the roofs go his eyes and outcry.

The French artist Jean Cocteau who was poet, playwright and film producer with an interest in the macabre and the occult, certainly understood that too close a contact with the mysteries supervised by the cat lead to inevitable death. Although 'The True Story of the Cat of Mr X' is a modern short story about the implacable jealousy of the female cat it is also about the goddess who wreaks vengeance upon those who do not properly worship her. It is the tale of a man who is called away unexpectedly to attend a funeral. He asks a neighbour to feed the cat in his absence. On his return he learns that the cat has not touched its food but has stayed in the bedroom all the while he was away. He thanks his neighbour and enters the house. Several days later Mr X is discovered dead in bed. The cat is still clinging to the man's neck and the throat opened by its claws still bleeds. The man's hands lie at his sides, he had not even attempted to defend himself.

That which made the sight insupportable was the certainty that his jealous lady, the cat, had played out a scene of charm and had waited until the unfaithful one had gone to his bed . . .

Thus the tale ends. The same theme of love for the old Mother-Goddess which in the end will bring destruction is to be found in a short story by the American playwright Tennessee Williams. Entitled 'The Malediction', it is about a man who feels bound to his source of comfort and support but in the end it is only the comfort of death which he finds. Alone in a strange city he adopts a stray cat:

> She was the first living creature in all of the strange northern city that seemed to answer the asking look in his eyes. She looked back at him with cordial recognition. Almost he could hear the cat pronouncing his name. 'Oh, so it's you, Lucio,' she seemed to be saying, 'I've sat here waiting for you a long, long time!'

He senses at once that a binding pact has been concluded. But he falls ill and has to go into hospital. When he returns to his lodgings he finds that his landlady has turned the cat out. He roams the streets till he finds her again, but she is injured and about to die. He walks to the river, the cat in his arms. At the river bank he speaks to her:

> 'Soon,' he whispered. 'Soon, soon, very soon.' Only a single instant she struggled against him: clawed his shoulder and arm in a moment of doubt. *My God, My God, why hast Thou forsaken me?* Then the ecstasy passed and her faith returned, they went away with the river. Away from the town, as the smoke, the wind took from the chimneys—completely away.

This tale and the previous one by Jean Cocteau are completely modern in style. One can detect an underlying identity of the cat with a goddess whose demands are inescapable but this aspect is not stressed and enjoyment of the story in no way depends on knowing about the myth.

This is even more true of the novel *Cat and Mouse* by the post-war German novelist, Gunter Grass. In this novel the cat makes one brief appearance. A group of schoolboys are lounging on the playing fields when:

A cat sauntered diagonally across the field and no one threw anything at it. A few of the boys were chewing or plucking at blades of grass. The cat belonged to the caretaker and was black. . . . It was a young cat, but no kitten. . . . The cat meandered about. . . . Through the grass stalks the caretaker's black cat showed a white bib. Mahlke was asleep. . . . The cat practised. Mahlke was asleep or seemed to be. I was next to him. . . . Still practising, the cat came closer. Mahlke's Adam's apple attracted attention because it was large, always in motion, and threw a shadow. Between me and Mahlke the caretaker's black cat tensed for a leap. We formed a triangle . . . for Mahlke's Adam's apple had become the cat's mouse. It was so young a cat, and Mahlke's whatsis was so active—in any case the cat leapt at Mahlke's neck; or I, . . . seized the cat and showed it Mahlke's mouse: and Joachim Mahlke let out a yell, but suffered only slight scratches.

And now it is up to me, who called your mouse to the attention of this cat and all cats, to write.

This description occurs in the first paragraph of the first chapter, and the cat is never mentioned again. Yet this one passage and the title of the book are enough to establish it as a presence throughout the novel. The hero of *Cat and Mouse* is a youth whose whole problem of adolescence and identity is symbolized by his grotesquely large and wobbly Adam's apple—his mouse. As the book progresses this becomes identified with his real self, even his soul. The young cat who mistakenly makes to pounce upon it is more than an ordinary cat. We are to understand that this is not an everyday cat involved in an isolated incident, but that 'this cat and all cats' stand for the destiny that will be placed upon Mahlke.

The setting of the novel is Danzig during World War II and the cat symbolizes the random, inconsequential quality of destiny. Mahlke always feels called upon to say and do things which draw attention to his mouse. He is determined to attract the notice of fate. At the end of the book when Mahlke disappears his friend does not know what has happened to him. One is left wondering whether his mouse-soul is now united with the fatal goddess whom during all his short life he courted.

While one would hesitate to describe Malcolm Lowry as the writer most typical of our time, his life and the topics he chose to write about are both heightened and extreme forms of the problems experienced by many today. Born and educated in England, he spent eighteen months at sea working as a deck hand. Then, after short stays in Paris and New York, he went to Mexico, which is the setting of his novel *Under the Volcano*. From Mexico he moved to the West Coast of Canada and lived and wrote in a small shack near Vancouver.

An alcoholic, writing was for Lowry an obsessive attempt to understand and resolve personal problems of identity. Continually searching for 'meanings' he was interested in Cabalism and at one time experimented with Voodoo. His writing consists of many layers of awareness, all of which are worked out with precise accuracy and attention to detail. It is therefore important for our purposes to look with care at the roles which cats play in his work.

At the end of his short novel called *Through the Panama* Malcolm Lowry describes a terrible Atlantic storm which threatens to break an old Liberty ship in two. At its very height 'Grisette' the captain's cat, comes on heat. One wonders if her name merely means 'little Grey', or in view of Lowry's constant preoccupation with drinking, whether it is intended to allude to the French verb *griser*—to intoxicate. Certainly her coming on heat seems to express her final drunken ecstasy at the force of the storm and recalls the World Serpent in disguise.

It soon becomes clear, however, that Malcolm Lowry is not merely re-telling old tales. During this appalling Atlantic crossing Lowry has his main character, who as in most of Lowry's writing is himself, jotting down notes for another book and describing a supposed painting by Hieronymous Bosch in which a man sets out from his home as a group of demons look down from a tree. One of these is a cat-like creature resembling, he says, the Cheshire Cat of Lewis Carroll. Lowry makes his fictional author speculate that the wretched man in the painting has not seen that his true destiny lies in remaining in the frightful hovel which is his home, but is setting out on some misguided quest watched by the demons in the tree. This is very like the situation of the two beggars in the play by W. B. Yeats where the blind beggar did not understand that in healing his infirmity he was losing an opportunity to attain another level of awareness. It was by accepting his infirmity that the lame beggar became 'blessed'. The cat is a silent witness to the scenes created by both Lowry and Yeats.

The short story called 'Present Estate of Pompeii' forms parts of the same sequence of writing as *Through the Panama*. In it Lowry describes a man named Wilderness who walks along a forest path in the dark with a cat:

> Once he stopped to pet the creature which suddenly seemed to him like some curious aspect or affection of eternity. . . .
> . . . Going through the forest that night with the bounding and whirling cat all at once it had seemed to him, as if he stood outside time altogether . . . that the whole damned thing was happening now, at this moment, continually repeating itself . . .

How very fitting that a man named Wilderness who goes along a forest path in the dark should have the insight that the cat stands for eternity. Lowry would have been completely aware that poetically it was right for the man's name to be Wilderness and that he should be going along a forest path at night when he had his sudden intuition of eternity. But the mythic or symbolic material has here been completely transformed and stated afresh.

Under the Volcano is without doubt Malcolm Lowry's masterpiece. In it, as in Gunter Grass's novel, a cat makes only one appearance. Yet this little animal is the only creature who is able to make real contact with the alienated, alcoholic Consul. She makes her entrance in Chapter 5 as he talks over the fence with Mr. Quincey, his disapproving neighbour:

> '—Hullo-hullo-look-who-comes-hullo-my-little-snake-in-the-grass-my-little-anguish-in-herba—' The Consul at this moment greeted Mr. Quincey's cat, momentarily forgetting its owner again as the grey, meditative animal, with a tail so long it

trailed on the ground, came stalking through the zinnias: he stopped, patting his thighs—'hello-pussy-my-little-Priapuss-puss, my-little-Oedipusspusspuss,' and the cat, recognizing a friend and uttering a cry of pleasure, wound through the fence and rubbed against the Consul's legs, purring. 'My little Xicotancatl.'

. . .

'. . . He's a character I've always liked. . . . William Blackstone. . . . Anyway, one day he arrived in what is now, I believe—no matter—somewhere in Massachusetts. And lived there quietly among the Indians. After a while the Puritans settled on the other side of the river. They invited him over; they said it was healthier on that side, you see. Ah, these people, these fellows with ideas,' he told the cat, 'old William didn't like them—no he didn't—so he went back to live among the Indians, so he did. But the Puritans found him out, Quincey, trust them. Then he disappeared altogether—God knows where. . . . *Now*, little cat,' the Consul tapped his chest indicatively, and the cat, its face swelling, body arched, important, stepped back, 'the Indians are in here.'

'They sure are,' sighed Mr. Quincey . . .

'Not real Indians. . . . And I didn't mean in the garden; but in *here*.' He tapped his chest again. 'Yes, just the final frontier of consciousness, that's all.'

When Quincey enquires after the Consul's friend and drinking partner Jacques Laruelle, it is as if:

Mr. Quincey's words knocked on his consciousness—or someone actually was knocking on a door—fell away, then knocked again, louder. Old De Quincey; the knocking on the gate in Macbeth. Knock, knock, knock: who's there? Cat. Cat who? Catastrophe. Catastrophe who? Catastrophysicist. What, is it you, my little popocat? Just wait an eternity till Jacques and I have finished murdering sleep? Katabasis to cat abysses . . . Of course, he should have known it, these were the final moments of the retiring of the human heart, and of the final entrance of the fiendish, the night insulated—. . .

The Consul walks back through his garden towards the house followed by the cat who is trying to catch an insect:

Then the behaviour of Mr. Quincey's cat began to fascinate him. The creature had at last caught the insect but instead of devouring it, she was holding its body, still uninjured, delicately between her teeth, while its lovely luminous wings, still beating, for the insect had not stopped flying an instant, protruded from either side of her whiskers, fanning them. The Consul stooped forward to the rescue. But the animal bounded just out of reach. He stooped again, with the same result. In this preposterous fashion, the Consul stooping, the cat dancing just out of reach, the insect still flying furiously in the cat's mouth, he approached his porch. Finally the cat extended a preparate paw for the kill, opening her mouth, and the insect, whose wings had never ceased to beat, suddenly and marvellously, flew out as might indeed the human soul from the jaws of death, flew up, up, up, soaring over the trees: . . .

'The grey meditative animal, with tail so long it trailed on the ground' sets the scene. It is 'snake-in-the-grass' and 'anguish in herba'. Oedipus could not escape his fate; Priapus, a son of Aphrodite and Dionysus was a jolly erotic fellow, a fertility god and a garden scarecrow; and Xicotancatl was an Aztec General who attempted to defend the old Aztec way of life against the invasion by Cortez and the Spaniards which would bring new religious ideas in its wake. Each of these characterizations of the cat draws attention to the fates which surround all of us. Oedipus wished to be a fully responsible man but was terribly humbled by the Gods. Xicotancatl opposed an inevitable historical development. Priapus, although a figure of fun, had a mother who was a Love-Goddess and a father who, as God of Wine, induced frenzied worship in his followers and punished those who would not worship him with madness. He therefore, like the Consul, is poised between the twin fates of being thought an amiable old fool and insanity.

Blackstone is described as having left White society to live among the Indians. But the Puritans attempt to get him to return saying it is healthier on their side of the river. Lowry makes us see that the Consul is in the same situation as Blackstone who withdrew across the river with the Indians. The Consul with the help of alcohol has withdrawn into the interior of his mind and does not wish to be rescued and rehabilitated by well-meaning commonsense people—'fellows with ideas'. Blackstone's response was to disappear altogether. It is the cat who the Consul tells this to and it seems to appreciate that 'the Indians are in here', within the Consul's heart. 'The final frontiers of consciousness' divide the real world from that primitive, prelogical area within. It is this area of the mind that the Consul, having as an alcoholic turned his back on the real world represented by the Puritans, tries to re-enter. The figure of Macbeth and 'knocking on the gate', mark a stage in his self-knowledge and progress towards inevitable doom and catastrophe. Beyond a certain point, self-awareness must always result in giving up the compromise which living in the real world involves: 'The final moments of the retiring of the human heart and the final entrance of the fiendish, the night insulated . . .' the heart gives up the attempt to man this frontier post and withdraws.

Then there follows a ludicrous scene. The cat catches an insect which remains alive, fluttering in its jaws. As the Consul attempts to release it they progress erratically along the path. This is life as the Consul knows it: he is the fragile hunted insect. Finally the cat opens its jaws and the insect 'suddenly and marvellously, . . . flew up, up, up, soaring over the trees:' This is more than release, it is transcendence. But the opposite outcome is also presented. 'Katabasis to cat abysses', a doom mediated by a cat. There is both knocking at the gate and ultimate release.

By such means as punning, enlisting the cat as confidante, making it with the insect in its jaws an arbiter of fate, and having it quietly look down while a man makes the wrong choices, Malcom Lowry has made of the cat a sympathetic but impartial observer of man's predicament, and a symbol of eternity.

The Consul's attempt to withdraw himself in defence against 'fellows with ideas' and the analogy of Blackstone's withdrawal across the river with the Indians reminds us not only of Freya's

Ninth World but also, in a curious way, of Alice's excursions down the rabbit-hole and through the mirror. Lowry has an animal similar to a Cheshire Cat look down upon the mistaken quest of wretched men in search of their destiny. Lewis Carroll's Cheshire Cat informs Alice that she would not have come to Wonderland unless she was mad, and yet this madness is also a quest whose pursuit may be as sane as the limited existence of the everyday world. As Robert Graves points out, when Alice returned she accepted her experiences:

> *As queer but true—not only in the main*
> *True, but as true as anything you'd swear to,*
> *The usual three dimensions you are heir to.*

Baudelaire and others, like Lowry and his character the Consul, tried to live life on both sides of the mirror. That their attempts ended disastrously is perhaps not surprising because the weight of society's disapproval was upon them. After the cat lost its protected position as a representative of deities in Egypt it has often been found associated with cults whose practitioners were on the defensive in a society which frowned upon their ways. 'A god among creatures—Yet also a stray like me' says the opening quotation to this chapter, and modern man in declining to live according to the precepts of organized belief has often, like the Consul, gone very far astray.

Now when we turn to look down the long avenue of time since the cat first walked unbidden into the granaries of Egypt we see that it has gone through many transformations in response to the changing circumstances of Europe's history. Besides being a practical asset as a hunter and a pet it has been the symbol for a bewildering variety of beliefs. Starting in Egypt as a representative of two religious ideas: a female lover, mother and destroyer goddess, and a male Sun-God and symbol of eternity, it was later transferred to Europe. There it became attached to female deities who were concerned with agriculture and both gave and took life, before being transformed into a Cat-King and the Devil's emissary. It was connected with attempts to balance good and evil in its identification with the serpent both in Egypt and in the north of Europe, and also as a symbol of the ambivalent moon. Today it is still popular as a pet and its symbolic potentialities may still be exploited by poets and writers who, in our secular society, have taken over from priests and priestesses the task of presenting symbolic truths.

What truths is the cat, as a symbol, likely to be called upon to convey? In the past we have seen that it has always been associated with attempts both to reconcile opposites and with eternity where, of course, the duality of opposition no longer exists. Whether thought of in terms of a life-giving and life-taking goddess, a Corn-Goddess who demands a sacrifice, a snake-cat duality, a moon which waxes and wanes or a Manichaean heresy, the cat has been a symbol which has encouraged man to face life as it is.

Can the cat symbol now help us to keep a balance between the nightmare which comes with the 'entrance of the fiendish; the night insulated' described by Malcolm Lowry and the happy realm of Lear and Carroll described as 'that lubberland of dream and laughter . . . where Apuleius pastured his Gold Ass' which Robert Graves points out is also ever present?

The curled cat in our homes still may represent eternity and, as Wilderness realized as he walked through the forest in the dark with a cat bounding at his side, 'the whole damned thing was happening now, at this moment, continually repeating itself . . .'

References to quotations

CHAPTER I

page

17 Rudyard Kipling. 'The Cat that Walked by Himself' in *Just So Stories*, p. 191. Macmillan and Co., London, 1955.

17 Voltaire. In *Life, History and Magic of the Cat* by Fernand Méry, p. 25. Paul Hamlyn, London, 1967.

19 Sir Ernest Budge. 'The Book of the Dead', vol. II, p. 390. Philip Lee Warner, London, 1913.

20 Sir Ernest Budge. *The Gods of the Egyptians*, vol. 1, p. 345. Methuen and Co. Ltd., London, 1904.

23 Sir Ernest Budge. *Liturgy of Funeral Offerings*, p. 53. Kegan Paul, Trench and Trübner and Co., London, 1909.

23 M. Oldfield Howey. *The Cat in the Mysteries of Religion and Magic*, pp. 151–152. Castle Books, N.Y., 1956.

24 *Diodorus Siculus I*, Book 1–11, 34, p. 285, translated by C. H. Oldfather. Loeb Classical Library, Harvard University Press: William Heinemann, London, 1933.

CHAPTER 2

27 Robert Herrick. In *A Dictionary of Cat Lovers* by Christabel Aberconway, p. 190. Michael Joseph, London, 1968.

31 'Bestiary' in *The Natural History of Cats* by Claire Necker, p. 78. A. S. Barnes and Co., Inc., S. Brunswick and N.Y., 1970.

32 'Republica' in *Proverbs in the Earlier English Drama* by Bartlett Jere Whiting, p. 112. Studies in Comparative Literature, vol. XIV, Octagon Books, N.Y., 1969.

34 'The Gwentian or South East Code' of Howel the Good. In *A Dictionary of Cat Lovers*, op. cit., p. 210.

page
35 Old Welsh Law. In Claire Necker, op. cit., p. 75.
35 Harleian MS. in F. C. Sillar and R. M. Meyler, *Cats Ancient and Modern*, p. 22. Studio Vista, London, 1966.
35 Italian proverb (traditional).
35 Franche Compté proverb. In Fernand Méry, op. cit., p. 40.
35 Sillar and Meyler, op. cit., p. 22.
36 *Demaundes Joyous: A Facsimile of the First English Riddle Book.* Edited by John Wardroper, p. 22. The Gordon Fraser Gallery Ltd., Bedford, 1971.
36 Geoffrey Chaucer. 'The Manciple's Tale'. In *The Canterbury Tales*, p. 504. A new translation by Nevill Coghill. Penguin Classics, Penguin Books, London, 1951.
36 The English Nunns' Rule. In Claire Necker, op. cit., p. 34.
37 Pangur Bán. Translated by Robin Flower. *Faber Book of Children's Verse*. Compiled by Janet Adam Smith, p. 70. Faber and Faber, London, 1953.

CHAPTER 3

40 William Brighty Rands. 'The Cat of Cats'. In *Oxford Book of Children's Verse* by Peter and Iona Opie, p. 236. Oxford University Press, London, 1973.
40 Anaxandrides of Rhodes. In Claire Necker, op. cit., p. 30.
45 Talmud. In M. Oldfield Howey, op. cit., p. 203.
46 M. Oldfield Howey, op. cit., p. 219.
46 Edward Topsell. In Sillar and Meyler, op. cit., p. 52.
47 Francis Barrett. In M. Oldfield Howey, op. cit., p. 203.
47 James G. Frazer. *The Golden Bough*, Abridged Edition, p. 32. Macmillan and Co., Ltd., London, 1933.
48 Marc de Vulson. In Claire Necker, op. cit., p. 148.
48 William Salmon. In Christabel Aberconway, op. cit., p. 455.
48 Père Evariste Huc, *The Chinese Empire*, vol. II, pp. 315–316. Longman, Brown, Green and Longmans, London, 1855.

CHAPTER 4

page

49 *Christopher Smart. Jubilate Agno*. Re-edited from the original manuscript with an introduction and notes by W. H. Bond, p. 116–118. Rupert Hart-Davis, London, 1954.

49 Sir Ernest Budge. 'Pistis Sophia', in *The Gods of the Egyptians*, vol. 1, op. cit., pp. 266–267.

50 *The Gospel of the Holy Twelve*, p. 6. Reprinted by John M. Watkins, London, 1956.

51 'The Book of Baruch' in *The Apocrypha*. An American translation by Edgar J. Goodspeed, p. 343. Vintage Books, Random House, N.Y., 1959.

52 Ibn Alalaf Abnaharwany. 'To a Cat Killed as she was Robbing a Dove-cote'. Translated by J. D. Carlyle in Claire Necker, op. cit., pp. 60–61.

54 Johann Wolfgang von Goethe. 'The West-East Divan'. XII Book of Paradise, p. 188. Translated by Prof. Dowden. J. M. Dent and Sons Ltd., London and Toronto, 1914.

CHAPTER 5

57 'A Magic Song of the Finns' in Claire Necker, op. cit., p. 19.

58 Peter Anker. *The Arts of Scandinavia*, vol. I, p. 253. Paul Hamlyn, London, 1970.

59 Lady Gregory. *Visions and Beliefs in the West of Ireland*, p. 291. The Coole Edition, Colin Smythe, Gerrards Cross, 1970.

59 Edward Topsell. In Sillar and Meyler, op. cit., p. 47.

60 *The International Maritime Dictionary*, edited by René de Kerchoue, pp. 131–132. 2nd edition. D. Van Norstrand Co., Princeton, 1961.

61 Otta F. Swire. *The Inner Hebrides and their Legends*, p. 78. Collins, Glasgow, 1964.

61 Katherine M. Briggs and Ruth L. Tongue. *Folk Tales of England*, p. 57. Routledge and Kegan Paul, London, 1965.

63 William Shakespeare. *Macbeth*. Act I, Scene III.

65 Robert Herrick. In Christabel Aberconway, op. cit., p. 190.

CHAPTER 6

page

67 William Morris. 'Lovers of Gudrun' in M. Oldfield Howey, op. cit., p. 58.

68 Peter Anker, op. cit., p. 98.

70 Sillar and Meyler, op. cit., p. 24.

73 Lady Gregory, op. cit., p. 290.

74 Fernand Méry, op. cit., p. 40.

74 May Eustace. *Mostly About Cats*, p. 72. Pelham Books, London, 1972.

74 Robert Graves. *The White Goddess*, p. 409. Paper Covered Edition. Faber and Faber, London, 1961.

CHAPTER 7

75 Anon. 'Nonsense Carol'. In *Oxford Book of Light Verse*. Chosen by W. H. Auden, pp. 87–88. Oxford University Press, London, 1938.

76 Briggs and Tongue, op. cit., pp. 46–47.

78 Enid Porter. *Cambridgeshire Customs and Folklore*, p. 161. Routledge and Kegan Paul, London, 1969.

78 John Gay. 'The Old Woman and Her Cats'. In M. Oldfield Howey, op. cit., pp. 188–189.

79 Julio Caro Baruja. *The World of the Witches*, pp. 229–230. Translated from the Spanish by Nigel Glendinning. Weidenfeld and Nicolson, London, 1964.

81 Fernand Méry, op. cit., p. 33.

81 Julio Carlo Baruja, op. cit., p. 76.

84 Margaret Murray. *The Witch-Cult of Western Europe*, pp. 234–235. Oxford Paperbacks, London, 1971.

84 Robert Graves, op. cit., p. 402.

85 Lady Gregory, op. cit., p. 291.

85 Briggs and Tongue, op. cit., pp. 59–60.

86 Isabel Gordon Carter. Journal of American Folklore, vol. 38, p. 544. 1925.

CHAPTER 8

page

90 Sir Walter Scott. In Sillar and Meyler, op. cit., p. 190.

91 Lady Gregory, op. cit., pp. 290–291.

92 Washington Irvine. In *Folklore and Folklife, an Introduction* by Richard M. Dorson, p. 472. University of Chicago Press, Chicago, 1972.

92 Katherine M. Briggs. *The Fairies in Tradition and Literature*, p. 72. Routledge and Kegan Paul, London, 1967.

93 Lady Gregory, op. cit., p. 291.

94 May Eustace, op. cit., p. 48.

94 Lady F. S. Wilde. *Ancient Legends, Mystic Charms and Superstitions*, pp. 24–30. London, 1887.

95 'Old Scottish writer' in M. Oldfield Howey, op. cit., p. 223.

96 Lady Gregory, op. cit., p. 292.

97 Katherine M. Briggs. *The Fairies in Tradition and Literature*, op. cit., p. 73.

97 Lady Gregory, op. cit., p. 169.

98 Lady Gregory, ibid., p. 257.

CHAPTER 9

100 Edward Lear. 'The Book of Nonsense'. In *Edward Lear's Nonsense Omnibus*. Frederick Warne, London, 1943.

101 *Sunday Express*, Jan. 13th 1929, in M. Oldfield Howey, op. cit., p. 120.

104 Albrighton Inn Sign, in M. Oldfield Howey, op. cit., p. 113.

104 Lady Gregory, op. cit., p. 290.

105 Lady Gregory, op. cit., p. 291.

105 W. B. Yeats. *Irish Fairy and Folk Tales*, edited by W. B. Yeats, p. 350 (note). Random House Modern Library, N.Y.

105 May Eustace, op. cit., p. 72.

106 M. Oldfield Howey, op. cit., p. 218.

106 M. Oldfield Howey, ibid., p. 217.

107 M. Oldfield Howey, ibid., p. 220.

108 Sillar and Meyler, op. cit., p. 42.

page

109   Christabel Aberconway, op. cit., pp. 189–190.

111   Briggs and Tongue, op. cit., pp. 105–106.

CHAPTER 10

113   Yogeśvara. In *Poems from the Sanskrit*. Translated by John
       Brough, p. 127. No. 222. Penguin Classics, Penguin
       Books, London, 1968.

116   Angelo de Gubernatis. *Zoological Mythology*, vol. II, pp. 64–
       65. Re-issued by Singer Tree Press, Book Tower, 1968.

116   Hindu Proverb. In Claire Necker, op. cit., p. 248.

117   *Poems from the Sanskrit*, op. cit., p. 74. No. 83.

117   *Poems from the Sanskrit*, ibid., p. 126. No. 218.

118   The Code of Manus. In *Zoological Mythology*, op. cit., p. 55
       (footnote).

119   Ovid. *Metamorphoses*. Translated by F. J. Miller. Book IX,
       vol. 11, p. 25. The Loeb Classical Library, Heinemann,
       London, 1916.

121   'Metamorphosis'. *Aesop's Fables*. Translated by S. A.
       Handford, p. 100, No. 96. Penguin Classics, Penguin
       Books, London, 1968.

122   Sillar and Meyler, op. cit., p. 22.

123   James O. Halliwell. *The Nursery Rhymes of England*, 2nd
       edition, p. 198. Bodley Head, London, 1970.

123   Peter and Iona Opie, op. cit., p. 172.

CHAPTER 11

125   James O. Halliwell. 'The Story of Catskin', op. cit., pp. 19–25.

129   Angelo de Gubernatis, op. cit., p. 55.

129   Bartlett Jere Whiting, op. cit., p. 89.

131   Angelo de Gubernatis, op. cit., p. 60.

CHAPTER 12

138   James O. Halliwell, op. cit., p. 60.

page
138 Halliwell, ibid., p. 14.
138 Halliwell, ibid., p. 13.
139 *Lavenders Blue. A Book of Nursery Rhymes.* Compiled by Kathleen Lines, p. 106. Oxford University Press, London, 1954.
140 Halliwell, op. cit., p. 196.
140 Halliwell, ibid., p. 170.
140 Halliwell, ibid., p. 171.
140 Halliwell, ibid., p. 170.
140 Halliwell, ibid., p. 171.
141 *Lavenders Blue*, op. cit., p. 148.
142 *Lavenders Blue*, ibid., p. 148.
143 Halliwell, op. cit., p. 223.
146 Halliwell, ibid., p. 25.
147 Sillar and Meyler, op. cit., p. 172.

CHAPTER 13

149 Mark Twain. In Fernand Méry, op. cit., p. 225.
150 La Fontaine. In Claire Necker, op. cit., pp. 56–57.
152 La Fontaine. In Claire Necker, ibid., p. 58.
152 *Christopher Smart. Jubilate Agno*, op. cit., pp. 116–118.
153 Christabel Aberconway, op. cit., p. 350.
154 Christabel Aberconway, ibid., p. 150.
154 Christabel Aberconway, ibid., pp. 298–300.
155 Heinrich Heine. 'The Witch' in Sillar and Meyler, op. cit., p. 65.
155 Heinrich Heine. Christabel Aberconway, op. cit., p. 181.
156 Peter and Iona Opie, op. cit., p. 268.
157 Thomas Hardy. 'Last Words to a Dumb Friend', The Poetical Works of Thomas Hardy, vol. I p. 622, Macmillan and Co., London, 1928.
157 Mrs. Gaskell. In Fernand Méry, op. cit., p. 224.
158 Giles Lytton Strachey. 'The Cat' in Christabel Aberconway, op. cit., p. 368.

page

159 Graham Tomson (*née* Rosamund Ball). 'To My Cat' in Christabel Aberconway, ibid., p. 391.

159 Oscar Wilde. In Claire Necker, op. cit., p. 175.

160 Algernon Swinburne. 'To a Cat' in Christabel Aberconway, op. cit., p. 371.

160 Théodore Gautier. In Christabel Aberconway, ibid., p. 47.

161 *Charles Baudelaire. 'Les Fleurs du Mal'*. Rendered into English by Alan Conder, p. 69. Cassell and Co., London, 1952.

162 Ibid., p. 70.

163 Ibid., p. 47.

164 Ibid., p. 62.

CHAPTER 14

167 Lewis Carroll. *Alice Through the Looking Glass*, p. 227. Macmillan and Co., 1968.

168 W. B. Yeats. *The Variorum Edition of the Plays of W. B. Yeats*. Edited by Russel K. Alspach, pp. 792–804. Macmillan and Co., London, 1966.

168 W. B. Yeats. Ibid., p. 805.

170 Kathleen Raine. *Defending Ancient Springs*, p. 125. Oxford University Press, London, 1967.

170 Edward Lear. 'The Owl and the Pussy Cat' in *Edward Lear's Nonsense Omnibus*, op. cit., p. 251.

172 Edward Lear. 'The Pobble Who has No Toes', ibid., p. 318.

173 Anon. 'Dame Wiggins of Lee' in *Oxford Book of Children's Verse* by Peter and Iona Opie, p. 153, op. cit.

174 Sir Edward Strachey's Introduction. *Edward Lear's Nonsense Omnibus*, op. cit.

175 Lewis Carroll. *Alice's Adventures in Wonderland*, p. 88. Puffin Story Books, Penguin Books, London, 1952.

176 Robert Graves. 'Alice' in *Collected Poems, 1959*, by Robert Graves, p. 49. Cassell and Co., London, 1959.

CHAPTER 15

page

179 Tony Ross. 'A Night Encounter with an Egyptian God' in *Children as Poets*. Edited by Denys Thomson, p. 63. Heinemann, London, 1972.

180 Sylvia Townsend Warner. 'The Traveller From the East and the Traveller From the West' in *The Cat's Cradle Book* by Sylvia Townsend Warner, pp. 139–140. Chatto and Windus, London, 1960.

181 Douglas Stewart. 'Frog Chorus' in *Stories and Verse*. Collected by F. J. Allsopp and O. W. Hunt, pp. 66–67. Angus and Robertson, Sydney, 1962.

183 Edith Sitwell. 'Dark Song' in *Taken Care Of* by Edith Sitwell, p. 48. Hutchinson, London, 1965.

183 Ted Hughes. 'Esther's Tom Cat' in *The Penguin Book of Animal Verse*. Introduced and edited by George MacBeth, pp. 59–60. Penguin Poets, Penguin Books, London, 1965.

184 Jean Cocteau. 'The Strange Story of the Cat of Mr X' in Fernand Méry, op. cit., p. 80.

185 Tennessee Williams. 'The Malediction' in *One Arm and Other Stories*, p. 33. New Directions, N.Y., 1945.

186 Gunter Grass. *Cat and Mouse*, pp. 5–6. Penguin Books, London, 1963.

188 Malcolm Lowry. 'The Present Estate of Pompeii' in *Hear Us O Lord from Heaven Thy Dwelling Place*, pp. 194–195. Penguin Books, 1969.

189 Malcolm Lowry. *Under the Volcano*, pp. 138–140 and p. 144. Penguin Modern Classics, Penguin Books, London, 1963.

192 Robert Graves. 'Alice', op. cit., p. 49.

Index

Index